PRINCIPLES OF
PUBLIC SPEAKING

DANTES/DSST* Test Study Guide

© 2020 Breely Crush Publishing, LLC

*DSST is a registered trademark of The Thomson Corporation and its affiliated companies, and does not endorse this book.

971021120143

Published by Breely Crush Publishing, LLC
10808 River Front Parkway
South Jordan, UT 84095
www.breelycrushpublishing.com

ISBN-10: 1-61433-675-X
ISBN-13: 978-1-61433-675-4

Printed and bound in the United States of America.

*DSST is a registered trademark of The Thomson Corporation and its affiliated companies, and does not endorse this book.

Table of Contents

Introduction to Public Speaking

Speaking in public is one of the things that people fear the most. However, public speaking can be both interesting and rewarding. Many people don't think to themselves, "I want a career as a public speaker!" and that's okay. Most public speakers do not become famous or well known because of their talent to form words or deliver pregnant pauses. Most public speakers that command $30,000 or more to speak are famous from their achievements in television, sports, politics or entertainment. So really, public speaking is not about a career or daydreaming about a large audience interested in what you have to say. Public speaking is an important communication tool that you will use in practical situations like at school, church, in a homeowner's association board meeting, or when giving a presentation at work.

There are three goals of conversation and public speaking:

- To inform
- To persuade
- To entertain

There are differences between public speaking and everyday conversation. Public speaking is much more structured. There are time limits on your speech and listeners don't interrupt. Public speaking is much more formal, you don't use jargon or bad grammar and as you practice the speech it evolves to the finished version that you will publicly present. Your posture and mannerisms are different when giving a speech than when you are chatting with a friend. You might fold clothes or fidget with your clothes while you chat, neither of which would be appropriate while giving a public speech.

Historical Aspects to Public Speaking

In Roman times, the Greeks and the Romans addressed each other and spoke for themselves in public trials and before government councils. They defined and studied public speaking in a systematic way. There have been many books written on the subject of public speaking. The most famous historical book was written by Aristotle entitled *Rhetoric*. Aristotle wanted to record the entire world and created 400 books. In his book *Rhetoric,* Aristotle wrote of two different proofs:

- Artistic
- Inartistic

Artistic proofs included:

- Ethos: the type of person that you are and your skills, i.e., education, values, speech delivery skills.

- Logos: appeals to the intellect.

- Pathos: appeals to the listener's passions, emotions, thoughts and wants.

The most important thing about public speaking is to be clear about getting your ideas across.

Ethics in Public Speaking

There are two sides to every story. Statistics can be manipulated to anyone's advantage. There is a flip side to every statistic. For example, take the following study on American pets.

- 45% of American households have a dog

- 20% have a cat and a dog

- 35% have no pets

- 15% have both a cat and a dog

The speaker would use the 45% statistic of information to prove that the dog is the most popular pet, while omitting the fact that 15% have both a cat *and* a dog – because those people were counted twice.

This is a simple example but it is important to realize that not every situation is black and white. There are many gray areas in law, politics and values. Also, context is important when it comes to determining a "gray" area. For example, there are three major groups of thought in the subject of abortion. Some believe that abortion is never morally correct, some believe that it is always morally correct, and some believe it is only acceptable in context, such as in cases of rape, incest or danger to the life of the mother.

Another large ethical issue in public speaking is plagiarism. Plagiarism is when you take someone else's work (for example, a written speech or essay) and claim it as your own. It can be as much as reading an entire speech not your own, patching together a speech from two or three sources (literally) or just not giving the correct credit to an anecdote or quote. It carries serious penalties in schools and in the professional public speaking arena, it will damage your reputation.

The Listening Process

The best speakers are great listeners. There are four parts of the listening process:

1. Sensing: seeing and listening

2. Attending: focusing on the listener (not traffic noise or a cell phone call)

3. Understanding: thinking about and understanding the words spoken

4. Remembering: fully understanding and recalling all the information presented

Guidelines for Listening

While each and every one of us thinks that we know what listening is, do we really? How many times have we been in an argument and been dying for the other person to shut up so we can say our next retort? How many times have we sat in a boring meeting and been so busy with our planner, our cell phone or our day dreams that even though our ears are hearing, we are so completely disengaged in the process that we are not really there? These are two easy examples of things that poor listeners do. And to become a good speaker, first we must become a good listener.

When you being a meeting or attending a speech or a sermon, you must prepare yourself to listen. Although this may sound obvious or an unnecessary step, it is the first and most important. This step involves putting your distractions away and becoming physically and mentally ready to receive the information. Next, we must stop talking and listen for others to give their points or even the responses to our own questions. Sometimes being silent in an interview situation can compel the other person to talk or elaborate more information. In fact, not talking can be a strategy used in negotiation. When you listen you must first decide your purpose. Is it to learn new information? Is it to criticize and critique a political position? Or is it simply for entertainment?

When you are a part of an audience, be open minded to what the speaker has to say. Take notes of things that interest you or things that you want to ask questions on after the speech is over. When you are open minded, you allow the speaker to try to convince you of his or her point of view. It is a delicate balance between being open minded and cautious of new ideas, until you decide the truth or fact of the matter with yourself.

The 90/10 Rule

The 90/10 rule was developed by teachers. Basically, it has to do with someone who is a poor public speaker and that they need to improve. This is based on the person themselves. For example, it is a positive trait to be authoritative. This helps you get things done, has people listen to you and helps you be a leader.

However, when you take this trait past 90%, the last 10% of the same trait can make them unbearable. The last 10% makes the person bossy and always have to have their way. This is when the first 90% of the trait is positive and the following 10% pushes the trait over the edge to become inappropriate or a poor communicator. Another example of this rule is someone that is easy going and speaks well in front of the group. However, they become SO casual that at times it appears that the subject is not important.

Choosing a Subject

There are a lot of great speech topics. Here are some great resources to find a topic or explore other ideas. Remember, the perfect topic for you is something that you are interested in and/or have experience in.

To pass the DANTES test you will need to give a *persuasive* speech. Almost any topic can be "flipped" or presented in a way that makes it a persuasive speech. As always, with a persuasive speech, you are taking a stand on an issue and trying to convince the listener of your point of view.

When you take the DANTES test, your topic will be assigned to you. However, you should take the time to prepare at least three different speeches (more on this later). When you choose your subject, try to avoid fixed beliefs such as politics or religion so you have the best chance of swaying minds in your 3-5 minute speech.

Think of at least 22 topics that you would be interested in giving a speech about. This is called brainstorming. Write down whatever comes to mind.

1.	12.
2.	13.
3.	14.
4.	15.
5.	16.
6.	17.
7.	18.
8.	19.
9.	20.
10.	21.
11.	22.

Some of you will have had a difficult time thinking about what would make an interesting speech. Now, looking at your list, can you see which of the ideas you wrote down are not truly persuasive? A persuasive speech needs to try to change the listener's mind about something. For example, I might have written that I feel confident about giving a speech about mosaics. This would be a great demonstrational topic because I could show how to plan, construct and install the project. However, it is not a great topic for a persuasive speech unless I can convert it to "cause friction" and try to persuade you, the listener, to change your mind or give you a different call to action. I could adapt my mosaic topic to be any of the following:

• Why mosaics are a lost art

• Why you need mosaics in your home

• Mosaics should be displayed in museums

• Mosaics should be taught in public school

Because the craft or art of mosaics is not very controversial, you have to use your imagination to determine an appropriate twist. You can "twist" anything you are interested in to become a great persuasion topic, although you will find that more controversial topics may have more research available to help you when researching your speech.

If you had a hard time thinking of a great topic, here are some websites that you can peruse for ideas. In addition, we've listed several topics below that can be formatted or adapted to your needs for this speech.

www.ehow.com
www.soyouwanna.com
www.mygoals.com

Various Speech Topics:
How to sew
How to grocery shop
How to scrapbook
How to fix a flat tire
How to put up shelves
How to create an exercise program
How to be a good waitress
How to make a birthday cake
How to make quesadillas
How to make potato salad
How to make a Thanksgiving turkey
How to prepare for college
How to improve your memory
How to take better notes
How to rock climb
How to save money on your electric bill
Job interviews
Vacations
Las Vegas
Disneyland/Disneyworld
Paris
London
New York
Rural America
Road trips
Golf
Volleyball
Basketball
Football
Baseball
Diet/weight loss
Voting
Airline safety
Email etiquette

Dating
Social media
Office politics
Rape and sexual assault
Drug abuse
Legalization of marijuana
Famous social and political figures
Environment
Pollution
Acid rain
Bottled water
Private school
Consumerism
Ethical advertising
World events
Traditions
Holidays (e.g., origins and activities)
Social security
Legal smoking age
Legal drinking age
Legal driving age
Legal marriage age
Compulsory school attendance
Speed limits
Town curfew
Arranged marriage
Care for the elderly
Why you should learn the guitar
Why you should vacation at….
Why you should travel to….
Why you should avoid…
Why you are…
Implications of the Do Not Call list
Spam
Adoption from third world countries
Death penalty (pro or con)
Death penalty for minors (pro or con)
Nuclear weapons (pro or con)
Social security should be abolished (pro or con)
Doctors should or should not be tested annually for AIDS
Every driver should have to take a test every three years (pro or con)
Public school students should have to study a foreign language (pro or con)
Marriage licenses should be renewable every five years (pro or con)

Select your topic from the list above or any that you think of and write it here. This will be your speech topic. We will be preparing and giving a small speech together later in the material.

(Example) Why the driving age should be raised to 18 years old.

Speech Topic:_____

Because we are giving a persuasive speech for the exam, our sample speech will be a persuasive speech topic.

Now that you have your topic, you must write your purpose statement. Your purpose statement is EXACTLY what you want to communicate. It must be a complete sentence phrased as a statement, NOT as a question. It also must be specific.

For example: Public school students should have to learn a foreign language.

Write your purpose statement here:

_____

Once you have determined your purpose statement, double check that it will work for your needs.

- Does it meet the assignment (persuasive in this case)?
- Do you have enough time to present it?
- Is the topic relevant to the audience?
- Is the topic important to you/the audience?

Now you will need to create a central idea. Many of you get that confused with the purpose statement. Your central idea is the EXACT statement of what you expect to say in your speech. This is your tag line, what you want the audience to remember about your speech.

Write your central idea here:

_____

Audience Analysis and Adaptation

You have to consider your audience in all aspects of your public speaking. What group are you speaking to? A group of school children, the Homeowners Association, the PTA, your peers, your manager? Each of these groups of people should be addressed in a very different way. You need to gear your topic, handouts, visual aids, jokes, and vocabulary tailored for the group that you are appealing to.

Demographics are statistical terms used to define a particular group. Demographics include but are not limited to:

- Gender
- Age
- Race/Ethnicity
- Income
- Education level

- Political attitudes and beliefs
- Religious beliefs (values)
- Occupation (job)
- Intelligence
- Geographic location

When analyzing your audience, don't forget that the audience will be analyzing you. Not only will they analyze your speech, but your accent, your clothes, the way you combed your hair and how you interact with the audience. While writing your speech, take into account your credibility and what the audience's expectations about the time and content will be of your speech.

Find out as much as you can in advance about your audience. Will it be made up for all female listeners? Parents? Children? Will they be 18-20 years old or 18-65? Knowing this information in advance will help you tailor your speech. You can get this information from the person that asked you to speak as well as how much time you will have and any suggested topics. In a classroom situation, take note of the demographics of your own class before you write your speech.

For the speech that you will give at the end of the test, consider who will be listening to your taped speech. You know that they will be a college level instructor. You don't know if they will be male or female. You have a general idea of the income level they are at because they will be an instructor from your own institution. You also know their education level. Knowing this in advance will help you prepare your mock speeches at home in preparation of test day.

You need to avoid ethnocentrism. What is ethnocentrism? It is the belief that your own culture or group is superior to other groups. For example, in a college setting, you may believe that your group of fraternity friends is inherently "better" or superior to other people on campus. This doesn't mean that you have to agree with other people's beliefs or values but that you accept them and work with those issues while formulating your speech. Generally, ethnocentrism is used in a racial context. Not only do you not want to be considered a bigot - but you have no idea the race or situation of the person that will be grading your speech. Just as you don't want to offend your audience with an off color joke, you don't want to offend the instructor who will decide if you pass or fail this DANTES test.

For the DANTES test, your REAL audience will be a college professor who will grade you according to a standard rubric but their personal preferences and prejudices will also play a part. Can you guess their age, gender, political party? No, not really in this testing situation. However, we do know that they are highly educated and informed. Your research will have to be compelling, interesting and original. They have heard many, many speeches over the years and while yours does not have to conclude with fireworks, they always help the grade.

For this DANTES test, we have told you that your grade will be determined by a college professor. However, the example test topic is the death penalty. You can choose to be pro or con on the topic. The audience is a public speaking class with male and female students ages 18 to 30.

Or you may assigned a topic such as term limits for political offices, whether sex education should be taught in school, is human cloning moral, do zoos help preserve and conserve the animal population?

Research

It's time to research your sample speech. It is going to be valuable to you to create your speech and follow along with the text. This will give you a much better understanding of the material and will really help you on your DANTES test.

You research a speech the same way that you would research a paper. Most likely, you have selected a speech topic which you know something about; as mentioned earlier, this will help you with the research. If you want to revise your topic, now's the time, before you begin your research.

Where do you find information for your speech? The following are excellent sources of information:

- Your brain

- The Internet, Google, etc.

- Interviewing people, experts

- Library

- Librarians

- Periodicals, Journals, and Magazines

When you need to do research, do it as soon as possible when you know you will have to be giving a speech. For DSST students, that time is now. Take the time to finish reading this section, then do your research for your sample topic.

Maslow's Hierarchy of Needs

Maslow's Hierarchy of needs consists of the following stages from the top down:

- Self-actualization
- Esteem needs
- Belonging and love
- Safety
- Physical needs

These stages begin at physical needs. First you need to have food, water, and shelter before you can worry about other requirements. Once those needs are met you may start to think of other necessities, such as safety. You might buy a gun or move to a more prosperous and safe area. Once you are fed, clothed and safe you will want to meet needs of belonging and love through relationships. If you feel loved, you may begin to think about your self-esteem and how you feel as a person, what you are contributing. The final stage, self-actualization, you may never meet. Most people do not.

Monroe's Motivational Sequence

Alan Monroe, a professor of speech, developed a motivational sequence that is perfect for policy speeches that are designed to inspire immediate action in the listeners. Monroe's Motivated Sequence is a detailed organizational pattern for speeches in which the desired result is to persuade the audience to take action.

There are five steps in the process, the first of which involves getting the audience's attention. In this step, it is necessary to convince the audience that they want to hear what the speaker has to say about the topic. The second step, called need, is describing or demonstrating a need or problem that the audience has. After the audience recognizes the need, the third step is for the speaker to introduce their solution to the problem. The speaker should specifically state what the audience would need to do. This step is called satisfaction. The fourth step is called visualization. In this step, the speaker describes the future benefits of their proposed solution. Finally, in the fifth step, the speaker calls the audience to action.

Here are the steps summarized:

1. Attention – gain the audience's attention

2. Need – make the audience feel ready for a change

3. Satisfaction – give them a solution to their want for change

4. Visualization – show them the benefits of the change

5. Action – tell the audience exactly what you want them to do

Primacy and Recency

Generally, the parts of a speech which the audience will most remember are the beginning and the end. This is why the concepts of primacy and recency are important in public speaking. Primacy refers to the fact that people will remember the things they hear first.

It is very important that a speaker's opening lines are clear and unambiguous about their point, because the audience is likely to assume that the first viewpoint they hear is the important or central viewpoint. The conclusion is also a central element of a speech. The closing arguments are even more important for a speaker to do well, because the first thing an audience remembers are the last things that they heard.

Recency is the opposite of primacy. You will begin with your weakest argument or points first and build up to your strongest argument.

 # Toulmin's Argument Model

Stephen Toulmin proposed that a practical argument must contain six different elements in order to be persuasive. These elements are claim, evidence, warrant, backing, qualifier and rebuttal. The claim is the statement which a speaker is arguing. It is what they wish to convince another person of. This is important in an argument because it builds a base from which to argue from and introduces the topic to the listener or audience.

The evidence is the proof used to convince the listener that the claim is valid and worth agreeing with. Generally, evidence comes in the form of data and facts. The warrant is a statement which connects the evidence with the claim and describes why the warrant proves the truthfulness of the claim.

Backing is additional information which proves that the warrant is correct, if a listener is not convinced by it. A qualifier is a statement which recognizes possible objections or problems relating to the claim. A rebuttal is used to convince the listener that the objections or problems are either irrelevant or that the benefits of the claim outweigh the objections to it.

Organizing Your Speech

The way that you organize your speech is very important. Speeches that are not easy to follow just confuse and bore the listeners and will not result in a passing grade. You outline a speech the same way you do a research paper, as shown.

- Introduction
- 1st main point
  - o Supporting evidence, story or example
  - o Supporting evidence, story or example
  - o Supporting evidence, story or example
  - o Transition
- 2nd main point
  - o Supporting evidence, story or example
  - o Supporting evidence, story or example
  - o Supporting evidence, story or example
  - o Transition
- 3rd main point
  - o Supporting evidence, story or example
  - o Supporting evidence, story or example
  - o Supporting evidence, story or example
  - o Transition
- Conclusion

Your introduction should be something that ties you in with the audience, either a story or joke, something to get their attention. This is also a time to establish your credibility.

Your credibility is what helps an audience believe what you are saying. It makes you an expert in their eyes. Sometimes you will experience a halo effect. An example of this is: you are an expert in the area of beekeeping but are giving a lecture about running a business. The audience transfers your expertise from beekeeping to business management.

After you have established your credibility, your introduction should end with your central idea and move into your first main point.

There are five types of main points:

- Chronological order (progressing through time, any how-to speech)

- Spatial order (progressing through a direction or pattern, showing the nature of how space is used such as in architecture, interior design, shelving, etc.)

- Causal order (showing a cause/effect relationship)

- Problem/solution order (first point shows the problem, the second the solution)

- Topical order (break the speech into subpoints)

There are four types of connectives/transitions:

- Transitions (In addition, let's now discuss…)

- Internal previews (Now that we've talked about the dangers of smoking around children, I will talk about the four contributions to delinquents…)

- Internal summaries (reminds listeners of what they just heard)

- Signposts (asking questions, showing where you are in a speech)

End your conclusion with a quotation, reinforce your main idea, drive your words home and leave your audience thinking about your speech when done.

When you look at a speech with this template, it does not seem so overwhelming. Each main point should have two to five pieces of supporting evidence, an example or an anecdote that proves the point. This is not the same outline that you would hand in to an instructor in a college class.

For the DANTES test you will not hand in your outline. Your outline will not be your complete speech written out; however, you can do that to get started. You'll need to think of three main points for your topic, which can be difficult. Complete this outline AS BEST YOU CAN for your sample speech. Put some effort into it!

- Introduction: _____

  _____

  _____

  _____

  _____

- 1st main point: _____

  ○ _____

  ○ _____

  ○ _____

  ○ Transition: _____

- 2nd main point: _____

  ○ _____

  ○ _____

  ○ _____

  ○ Transition: _____

- 3rd main point: _____

  ○ _____

  ○ _____

  ○ _____

  ○ Transition: _____

- Conclusion: _____

  _____

  _____

  _____

  _____

Your speech needs to be about **four minutes** long. Try giving your speech aloud with a tape recorder and looking at yourself in the mirror. Play it back to hear your stumbles or weaknesses.

You should practice until you feel very comfortable and you can deliver the speech fluidly and in the time provided. It is an automatic failure to be **less than three minutes or longer than five minutes**. Make sure you practice to that four minute mark. When you have done your speech five or six times, ask a friend or family member to listen to your speech and give you feedback.

Persuasive Speech

There are three main types of persuasive speeches:

1. Questions of Fact

2. Questions of Value

3. Questions of Policy

QUESTIONS OF FACT

A question of fact is a statement that can be proven true or false. Some examples are:

How many miles is it from my house to campus?
How many games has our local sports team won in the past year?
How many have they ever won?

Questions of fact can easily be summed up into "how much?" and "how many?." These types of questions are black and white. There is a certified answer. It could be found online, or in Mapquest, but there is one answer. The answer is either right or wrong. However, there are some issues that are questions of fact. These are more tricky because the answer is out there, we just may not know what it is, but there is an answer. Examples of this type of question would be:

•   What happened to Roanoke?

•   What happened to the Aztecs?

•   What causes cancer?

If you are giving an informative speech and your aim is to provide the information as non-biased as possible, it will be considered **nonpartisan**. If you are giving a persuasive speech regarding a question of fact, you are **partisan**.

QUESTION OF VALUE

A question of value is about the morality, rightness, wrongness, worth, etc., of an idea or action. Basically, a question of value is any question where **values** are used to determine a speaker's and a listener's position.

QUESTION OF POLICY

A question of policy is whether or not a specific action should or should not be taken. Questions of policy usually involve the word "should" in their statement. For example:

- Should social security receive more funding?

- Should teachers be given a raise?

- Should we institute a driving test for the elderly?

With a question of policy, you are trying to either gain passive agreement or immediate action.

Types of Reasoning

There are four types of reasoning:

- Deductive – using a general conclusion to support a specific argument.

- Inductive – using specific cases to support a general conclusion.

- Analogical – reasoning by analogy.

- Causal – implying a link between two items, ideas, etc.

 # Reasoning Fallacies

What is a fallacy? A fallacy is a false conception based on faulty reasoning. Basically, it is a solution or a theory based on inaccurate information or "proof" in the argument. The following are the most common fallacies in arguments. Make sure that your speeches do not include this type of reasoning.

- Hasty Generalization
  — When you draw a conclusion based on a sample group that is too small. For example, because one local mother said to be homeschooling her children did not do so at all, you are advocating that homeschooling should not be allowed in the state.

- Begging the Question (also called circular reasoning)
  — This is when "it is what it is" – for example, Tom is a good driver because he never gets any tickets.

- Slippery Slope
  — This is when you assume that when one thing happens, it will create a domino effect. For example, we don't dare to have a television because then soon our children would become devoid of original thought.

- Red Herring
  — This is where you introduce unrelated information that misdirects the attention (usually to enlist the support of the audience) while it confuses the original problem or issue. For example, "Guns don't kill people; people kill people" takes the attention away from the primary issue, gun control, and shifts the attention to murder and other social issues.

- False Division (false dichotomy, also known as either/or)
  — This is when you have created an "either/or" where there wasn't one before. For example, the statement "you are either pro-life or a murderer" and "cut government spending or raise taxes" are both false division arguments.

- Non-sequitur
  — This is when the conclusion does not relate to the proof or evidence. An example of a non-sequitur is "post hoc, ergo propter hoc" which is translated to be "after this, therefore because of this." An example of this would be, I have been 40 pounds overweight for years. I started taking ABC formula and six weeks later, I had lost 35 pounds and found a new boyfriend.

- Ad Populum
  — This is an argument that uses popular opinion as justification, usually with a small sample. For example, four out of five dentists choose Trident.

- Ad Hominem
  — When you attack the person raising an issue, not the issue itself.

- Ad Ignoratiam
  — When you insist something is true because no one can prove it as false. For example, because no one has disproven that there is life after death, there must be.

- Analogical Fallacy
  — Assuming that two things that are similar are equal. For example, he is an excellent tennis player; he must be wonderful at golf.

Delivering Your Presentation

When delivering your presentation, there are many things to consider. You must make your voice strong and interesting, not too loud, but loud enough to be heard. You should speak with conviction, as if you believe (and you should believe) the main points of your presentation. You need to manage your nervousness. It is normal to feel uncomfortable when giving your first speech. You will overcome this by practicing. The more you practice your speech, the more comfortable you will become. When practicing for your DANTES speech, record it with a tape recorder. Give your speech all the way through without stopping. Yes, there may be times when you stumble over your words or lose your train of thought. Don't start over because you are also teaching yourself to recover quickly from those slips and to feel comfortable with the material you are presenting.

In a regular classroom setting, the list would go on and on of what you should do, wear and visual aids you should prepare. We're only focusing on what you need to do to pass your DANTES test.

One more thing to do while taping your sample speech and your TEST speech is to SMILE! You may not believe it now, but you sound different on the phone when you SMILE. You'll sound more confident on the tape which should help you receive a better score.

Don't Do These Things

Here are some things to NOT do in a speech:

- Make racial comments or jokes
- Make sexist comments or jokes
- Use abbreviations
- Eat food
- Drink water
- Chew gum
- Avoid eye contact
- Shuffle papers
- Fidget
- Sway back and forth
- Sit down

Historical Speeches

PATRICK HENRY'S "GIVE ME LIBERTY OR GIVE ME DEATH"

No man thinks more highly than I do of the patriotism, as well as abilities, of the very worthy gentlemen who have just addressed the House. But different men often see the same subject in different lights; and, therefore, I hope it will not be thought disrespectful to those gentlemen if, entertaining as I do opinions of a character very opposite to theirs, I shall speak forth my sentiments freely and without reserve. This is no time for ceremony. The questing before the House is one of awful moment to this country. For my own part, I consider it as nothing less than a question of freedom or slavery; and in proportion to the magnitude of the subject ought to be the freedom of the debate. It is only in this way that we can hope to arrive at truth, and fulfill the great responsibility which we hold to God and our country. Should I keep back my opinions at such a time, through fear of giving offense, I should consider myself as guilty of treason towards my country, and of an act of disloyalty toward the Majesty of Heaven, which I revere above all earthly kings.

Mr. President, it is natural to man to indulge in the illusions of hope. We are apt to shut our eyes against a painful truth, and listen to the song of that siren till she transforms us into beasts. Is this the part of wise men, engaged in a great and arduous struggle for liberty? Are we disposed to be of the number of those who, having eyes, see not, and, having ears, hear not, the things which so nearly concern their temporal salvation? For my part, whatever anguish of spirit it may cost, I am willing to know the whole truth; to know the worst, and to provide for it.

I have but one lamp by which my feet are guided, and that is the lamp of experience. I know of no way of judging of the future but by the past. And judging by the past, I wish to know what there has been in the conduct of the British ministry for the last ten years to justify those hopes with which gentlemen have been pleased to solace themselves and the House. Is it that insidious smile with which our petition has been lately received? Trust it not, sir; it will prove a snare to your feet. Suffer not yourselves to be betrayed with a kiss. Ask yourselves how this gracious reception of our petition comports with those warlike preparations which cover our waters and darken our land. Are fleets and armies necessary to a work of love and reconciliation? Have we shown ourselves so unwilling to be reconciled that force must be called in to win back our love? Let us not deceive ourselves, sir. These are the implements of war and subjugation; the last arguments to which kings resort. I ask gentlemen, sir, what means this martial array, if its purpose be not to force us to submission? Can gentlemen assign any other possible motive for it? Has Great Britain any enemy, in this quarter of the world, to call for all this accumulation of navies and armies? No, sir, she has none. They are meant for us: they can be meant for no other. They are sent over to bind and rivet upon us those chains which the British ministry have been so long forging. And what have we to oppose to them?

Shall we try argument? Sir, we have been trying that for the last ten years. Have we anything new to offer upon the subject? Nothing. We have held the subject up in every light of which it is capable; but it has been all in vain. Shall we resort to entreaty and humble supplication? What terms shall we find which have not been already exhausted? Let us not, I beseech you, sir, deceive ourselves. Sir, we have done everything that could be done to avert the storm which is now coming on. We have petitioned; we have remonstrated; we have supplicated; we have prostrated ourselves before the throne, and have implored its interposition to arrest the tyrannical hands of the ministry and Parliament. Our petitions have been slighted; our remonstrances have produced additional violence and insult; our supplications have been disregarded; and we have been spurned, with contempt, from the foot of the throne! In vain, after these things, may we indulge the fond hope of peace and reconciliation. There is no longer any room for hope. If we wish to be free -- if we mean to preserve inviolate those inestimable privileges for which we have been so long contending--if we mean not basely to abandon the noble struggle in which we have been so long engaged, and which we have pledged ourselves never to abandon until the glorious object of our contest shall be obtained -- we must fight! I repeat it, sir, we must fight! An appeal to arms and to the God of hosts is all that is left us!

They tell us, sir, that we are weak; unable to cope with so formidable an adversary. But when shall we be stronger? Will it be the next week, or the next year? Will it be when we are totally disarmed, and when a British guard shall be stationed in every house?

Shall we gather strength by irresolution and inaction? Shall we acquire the means of effectual resistance by lying supinely on our backs and hugging the delusive phantom of hope, until our enemies shall have bound us hand and foot? Sir, we are not weak if we make a proper use of those means which the God of nature hath placed in our power. The millions of people, armed in the holy cause of liberty, and in such a country as that which we possess, are invincible by any force which our enemy can send against us. Besides, sir, we shall not fight our battles alone. There is a just God who presides over the destinies of nations, and who will raise up friends to fight our battles for us. The battle, sir, is not to the strong alone; it is to the vigilant, the active, the brave. Besides, sir, we have no election. If we were base enough to desire it, it is now too late to retire from the contest. There is no retreat but in submission and slavery! Our chains are forged! Their clanking may be heard on the plains of Boston! The war is inevitable -- and let it come! I repeat it, sir, let it come.

It is in vain, sir, to extenuate the matter. Gentlemen may cry, Peace, Peace -- but there is no peace. The war is actually begun! The next gale that sweeps from the north will bring to our ears the clash of resounding arms! Our brethren are already in the field! Why stand we here idle? What is it that gentlemen wish? What would they have? Is life so dear, or peace so sweet, as to be purchased at the price of chains and slavery? Forbid it, Almighty God! I know not what course others may take; but as for me, give me liberty or give me death!

MARTIN LUTHER KING JR.'S SPEECH "I HAVE A DREAM" CAN BE HEARD AND READ AT: http://www.americanrhetoric.com/speeches/mlkihaveadream.htm

RONALD REAGAN'S THE SPACE SHUTTLE "CHALLENGER" TRAGEDY ADDRESS

Ladies and Gentlemen, I'd planned to speak to you tonight to report on the state of the Union, but the events of earlier today have led me to change those plans. Today is a day for mourning and remembering. Nancy and I are pained to the core by the tragedy of the shuttle Challenger. We know we share this pain with all of the people of our country. This is truly a national loss.

Nineteen years ago, almost to the day, we lost three astronauts in a terrible accident on the ground. But we've never lost an astronaut in flight. We've never had a tragedy like this. And perhaps we've forgotten the courage it took for the crew of the shuttle. But they, the Challenger Seven, were aware of the dangers, but overcame them and did their jobs brilliantly. We mourn seven heroes: Michael Smith, Dick Scobee, Judith Resnik, Ronald McNair, Ellison Onizuka, Gregory Jarvis, and Christa McAuliffe. We mourn their loss as a nation together.

For the families of the seven, we cannot bear, as you do, the full impact of this tragedy. But we feel the loss, and we're thinking about you so very much. Your loved ones were daring and brave, and they had that special grace, that special spirit that says, "Give me a challenge, and I'll meet it with joy." They had a hunger to explore the universe and discover its truths. They wished to serve, and they did. They served all of us.

We've grown used to wonders in this century. It's hard to dazzle us. But for twenty-five years the United States space program has been doing just that. We've grown used to the idea of space, and, perhaps we forget that we've only just begun. We're still pioneers. They, the members of the Challenger crew, were pioneers.

And I want to say something to the schoolchildren of America who were watching the live coverage of the shuttle's take-off. I know it's hard to understand, but sometimes painful things like this happen. It's all part of the process of exploration and discovery. It's all part of taking a chance and expanding man's horizons. The future doesn't belong to the fainthearted; it belongs to the brave. The Challenger crew was pulling us into the future, and we'll continue to follow them.

I've always had great faith in and respect for our space program. And what happened today does nothing to diminish it. We don't hide our space program. We don't keep secrets and cover things up. We do it all up front and in public. That's the way freedom is, and we wouldn't change it for a minute.

We'll continue our quest in space. There will be more shuttle flights and more shuttle crews and, yes, more volunteers, more civilians, more teachers in space. Nothing ends here; our hopes and our journeys continue.

I want to add that I wish I could talk to every man and woman who works for NASA, or who worked on this mission and tell them: "Your dedication and professionalism have moved and impressed us for decades. And we know of your anguish. We share it."

There's a coincidence today. On this day three hundred and ninety years ago, the great explorer Sir Francis Drake died aboard ship off the coast of Panama. In his lifetime the great frontiers were the oceans, and a historian later said, "He lived by the sea, died on it, and was buried in it." Well, today, we can say of the Challenger crew: Their dedication was, like Drake's, complete.

The crew of the space shuttle Challenger honored us by the manner in which they lived their lives. We will never forget them, nor the last time we saw them, this morning, as they prepared for their journey and waved goodbye and "slipped the surly bonds of earth" to "touch the face of God."

Thank you.

GEORGE W. BUSH: 2004 PRESIDENTIAL ELECTION VICTORY SPEECH

Thank you all. Thank you all for coming. We had a long night, and a great night.

The voters turned out in record numbers and delivered an historic victory.

Earlier today, Senator Kerry called with his congratulations. We had a really good phone call. He was very gracious. Senator Kerry waged a spirited campaign, and he and his supporters can be proud of their efforts. Laura and I wish Senator Kerry and Teresa and their whole family all our best wishes.

America has spoken, and I'm humbled by the trust and the confidence of my fellow citizens. With that trust comes a duty to serve all Americans, and I will do my best to fulfill that duty every day as your President.

There are many people to thank, and my family comes first.

Laura is the love of my life. I'm glad you love her, too.

I want to thank our daughters, who joined their dad for his last campaign.

I appreciate the hard work of my sister and my brothers.

I especially want to thank my parents for their loving support.

I'm grateful to the Vice-President and Lynne and their daughters, who have worked so hard and been such a vital part of our team. The Vice-President serves America with wisdom and honor, and I'm proud to serve beside him.

I want to thank my superb campaign team. I want to thank you all for your hard work. I was impressed every day by how hard and how skillful our team was.

I want to thank our chairman Mark Racicot; the campaign manager, Ken Mehlman; the architect, Karl Rove.

I want to thank Ed Gillespie for leading our Party so well.

I want to thank the thousands of our supporters across our country. I want to thank you for your hugs on the rope lines. I want to thank you for your prayers on the rope lines. I want to thank you for your kind words on the rope lines. I want to thank you for everything you did to make the calls and to put up the signs, to talk to your neighbors, and to get out the vote.

And because you did the incredible work, we are celebrating today.

There's an old saying, "Do not pray for tasks equal to your powers; pray for powers equal to your tasks."

In four historic years, America has been given great tasks and faced them with strength and courage.

Our people have restored the vigor of this economy and shown resolve and patience in a new kind of war.

Our military has brought justice to the enemy and honor to America.

Our nation -- Our nation has defended itself and served the freedom of all mankind. I'm proud to lead such an amazing country, and I am proud to lead it forward.

Because we have done the hard work, we are entering a season of hope. We'll continue our economic progress.

We'll reform our outdated tax code. We'll strengthen the Social Security for the next generation.

We'll make public schools all they can be, and we will uphold our deepest values of family and faith.

We'll help the emerging democracies of Iraq and Afghanistan, so they can grow in strength and defend their freedom, and then our servicemen and women will come home with the honor they have earned.

With good allies at our side, we will fight this war on terror with every resource of our national power, so our children can live in freedom and in peace.

Reaching these goals will require the broad support of Americans, so today I want to speak to every person who voted for my opponent. To make this nation stronger and better, I will need your support and I will work to earn it. I will do all I can do to deserve your trust.

A new term is a new opportunity to reach out to the whole nation. We have one country, one constitution, and one future that binds us. And when we come together and work together, there is no limit to the greatness of America.

Let me close with a word to the people of the state of Texas. We have known each other the longest, and you started me on this journey. On the open plains of Texas, I first learned the character of our country -- sturdy and honest, and as hopeful as the break of day. I will always be grateful to the good people of my State. And whatever the road that lies ahead, that road will take me home.

A campaign has ended, and the United States of America goes forward with confidence and faith. I see a great day coming for our country, and I am eager for the work ahead. God bless you. And may God bless America.

FRANKLIN DELANO ROOSEVELT: PEARL HARBOR ADDRESS TO THE NATION - DECEMBER 8, 1941

Mr. Vice President, Mr. Speaker, Members of the Senate, and of the House of Representatives:

Yesterday, December 7th, 1941 -- a date which will live in infamy -- the United States of America was suddenly and deliberately attacked by naval and air forces of the Empire of Japan.

The United States was at peace with that nation and, at the solicitation of Japan, was still in conversation with its government and its emperor looking toward the maintenance of peace in the Pacific.

Indeed, one hour after Japanese air squadrons had commenced bombing in the American island of Oahu, the Japanese ambassador to the United States and his colleague delivered to our Secretary of State a formal reply to a recent American message. And while this reply stated that it seemed useless to continue the existing diplomatic negotiations, it contained no threat or hint of war or of armed attack.

It will be recorded that the distance of Hawaii from Japan makes it obvious that the attack was deliberately planned many days or even weeks ago. During the intervening time, the Japanese government has deliberately sought to deceive the United States by false statements and expressions of hope for continued peace.

The attack yesterday on the Hawaiian islands has caused severe damage to American naval and military forces. I regret to tell you that very many American lives have been lost. In addition, American ships have been reported torpedoed on the high seas between San Francisco and Honolulu.

Yesterday, the Japanese government also launched an attack against Malaya.

Last night, Japanese forces attacked Hong Kong.

Last night, Japanese forces attacked Guam.

Last night, Japanese forces attacked the Philippine Islands.

Last night, the Japanese attacked Wake Island.

And this morning, the Japanese attacked Midway Island.

Japan has, therefore, undertaken a surprise offensive extending throughout the Pacific area. The facts of yesterday and today speak for themselves. The people of the United States have already formed their opinions and well understand the implications to the very life and safety of our nation.

As commander in chief of the Army and Navy, I have directed that all measures be taken for our defense. But always will our whole nation remember the character of the onslaught against us.

No matter how long it may take us to overcome this premeditated invasion, the American people in their righteous might will win through to absolute victory.

I believe that I interpret the will of the Congress and of the people when I assert that we will not only defend ourselves to the uttermost, but will make it very certain that this form of treachery shall never again endanger us.

Hostilities exist. There is no blinking at the fact that our people, our territory, and our interests are in grave danger.

With confidence in our armed forces, with the unbounding determination of our people, we will gain the inevitable triumph -- so help us God.

I ask that the Congress declare that since the unprovoked and dastardly attack by Japan on Sunday, December 7th, 1941, a state of war has existed between the United States and the Japanese empire.

PRESIDENT GEORGE W. BUSH 9/11 SPEECH, DELIVERED 9/20/01

Mr. Speaker, Mr. President Pro Tempore, members of Congress, and fellow Americans:

In the normal course of events, Presidents come to this chamber to report on the state of the Union. Tonight, no such report is needed. It has already been delivered by the American people.

We have seen it in the courage of passengers, who rushed terrorists to save others on the ground -- passengers like an exceptional man named Todd Beamer. And would you please help me to welcome his wife, Lisa Beamer, here tonight. We have seen the state of our Union in the endurance of rescuers, working past exhaustion. We've seen the unfurling of flags, the lighting of candles, the giving of blood, the saying of prayers -- in English, Hebrew, and Arabic. We have seen the decency of a loving and giving people who have made the grief of strangers their own. My fellow citizens, for the last nine days, the entire world has seen for itself the state of our Union -- and it is strong.

Tonight we are a country awakened to danger and called to defend freedom. Our grief has turned to anger, and anger to resolution. Whether we bring our enemies to justice, or bring justice to our enemies, justice will be done. I thank the Congress for its leadership at such an important time. All of America was touched on the evening of the tragedy to see Republicans and Democrats joined together on the steps of this Capitol, singing "God Bless America." And you did more than sing; you acted, by delivering 40 billion dollars to rebuild our communities and meet the needs of our military. Speaker Hastert, Minority Leader Gephardt, Majority Leader Daschle, and Senator Lott, I thank you for your friendship, for your leadership, and for your service to our country. And on behalf of the American people, I thank the world for its outpouring of support. America will never forget the sounds of our National Anthem playing at Buckingham Palace, on the streets of Paris, and at Berlin's Brandenburg Gate.

We will not forget South Korean children gathering to pray outside our embassy in Seoul, or the prayers of sympathy offered at a mosque in Cairo. We will not forget moments of silence and days of mourning in Australia and Africa and Latin America. Nor will we forget the citizens of 80 other nations who died with our own: dozens of Pakistanis; more than 130 Israelis; more than 250 citizens of India; men and women from El Salvador, Iran, Mexico, and Japan; and hundreds of British citizens. America has no truer friend than Great Britain. Once again, we are joined together in a great cause -- so honored the British Prime Minister has crossed an ocean to show his unity with America. Thank you for coming, friend.

On September the 11th, enemies of freedom committed an act of war against our country. Americans have known wars -- but for the past 136 years, they have been wars on foreign soil, except for one Sunday in 1941. Americans have known the casualties of war -- but not at the center of a great city on a peaceful morning. Americans have known surprise attacks -- but never before on thousands of civilians. All of this was brought upon us in a single day -- and night fell on a different world, a world where freedom itself is under attack. Americans have many questions tonight. Americans are asking: Who attacked our country? The evidence we have gathered all points to a collection of loosely affiliated terrorist organizations known as al Qaeda. They are some of the murderers indicted for bombing American embassies in Tanzania and Kenya, and responsible for bombing the USS Cole. Al Qaeda is to terror what the mafia is to crime. But its goal is not making money; its goal is remaking the world -- and imposing its radical beliefs on people everywhere.

The terrorists practice a fringe form of Islamic extremism that has been rejected by Muslim scholars and the vast majority of Muslim clerics, a fringe movement that perverts the peaceful teachings of Islam. The terrorists' directive commands them to kill Christians and Jews, to kill all Americans, and make no distinctions among military and civilians, including women and children. This group and its leader -- a person named Usama bin Laden -- are linked to many other organizations in different countries, including the Egyptian Islamic Jihad and the Islamic Movement of Uzbekistan. There are thousands of these terrorists in more than 60 countries. They are recruited from their own nations and neighborhoods and brought to camps in places like Afghanistan, where they are trained in the tactics of terror. They are sent back to their homes or sent to hide in countries around the world to plot evil and destruction.

The leadership of al Qaeda has great influence in Afghanistan and supports the Taliban regime in controlling most of that country. In Afghanistan, we see al Qaeda's vision for the world. Afghanistan's people have been brutalized; many are starving and many have fled. Women are not allowed to attend school. You can be jailed for owning a television. Religion can be practiced only as their leaders dictate. A man can be jailed in Afghanistan if his beard is not long enough.

The United States respects the people of Afghanistan. After all, we are currently its largest source of humanitarian aid; but we condemn the Taliban regime. It is not only repressing its own people, it is threatening people everywhere by sponsoring and sheltering and supplying terrorists. By aiding and abetting murder, the Taliban regime is committing murder.

And tonight, the United States of America makes the following demands on the Taliban: Deliver to United States authorities all the leaders of al Qaeda who hide in your land. Release all foreign nationals, including American citizens, you have unjustly imprisoned. Protect foreign journalists, diplomats, and aid workers in your country. Close immediately and permanently every terrorist training camp in Afghanistan, and hand over every terrorist, and every person in their support structure, to appropriate authorities. Give the United States full access to terrorist training camps, so we can make sure they are no longer operating. These demands are not open to negotiation or discussion. The Taliban must act, and act immediately. They will hand over the terrorists, or they will share in their fate.

I also want to speak tonight directly to Muslims throughout the world. We respect your faith. It's practiced freely by many millions of Americans, and by millions more in countries that America counts as friends. Its teachings are good and peaceful, and those who commit evil in the name of Allah blaspheme the name of Allah. The terrorists are traitors to their own faith, trying, in effect, to hijack Islam itself. The enemy of America is not our many Muslim friends; it is not our many Arab friends. Our enemy is a radical network of terrorists, and every government that supports them. Our war on terror begins with al Qaeda, but it does not end there. It will not end until every terrorist group of global reach has been found, stopped, and defeated.

Americans are asking, why do they hate us? They hate what they see right here in this chamber -- a democratically elected government. Their leaders are self-appointed. They hate our freedoms -- our freedom of religion, our freedom of speech, our freedom to vote and assemble and disagree with each other. They want to overthrow existing governments in many Muslim countries, such as Egypt, Saudi Arabia, and Jordan. They want to drive Israel out of the Middle East. They want to drive Christians and Jews out of vast regions of Asia and Africa. These terrorists kill not merely to end lives, but to disrupt and end a way of life. With every atrocity, they hope that America grows fearful, retreating from the world and forsaking our friends. They stand against us, because we stand in their way.

We are not deceived by their pretenses to piety. We have seen their kind before. They are the heirs of all the murderous ideologies of the 20th century. By sacrificing human life to serve their radical visions -- by abandoning every value except the will to power -- they follow in the path of fascism, Nazism, and totalitarianism. And they will follow that path all the way, to where it ends: in history's unmarked grave of discarded lies. Americans are asking: How will we fight and win this war? We will direct every resource at our command -- every means of diplomacy, every tool of intelligence, every instrument of law enforcement, every financial influence, and every necessary weapon of war -- to the disruption and to the defeat of the global terror network.

Now this war will not be like the war against Iraq a decade ago, with a decisive liberation of territory and a swift conclusion. It will not look like the air war above Kosovo two years ago, where no ground troops were used and not a single American was lost in combat. Our response involves far more than instant retaliation and isolated strikes. Americans should not expect one battle, but a lengthy campaign, unlike any other we have ever seen. It may include dramatic strikes, visible on TV, and covert operations, secret even in success. We will starve terrorists of funding, turn them one against another, drive them from place to place, until there is no refuge or no rest. And we will pursue nations that provide aid or safe haven to terrorism. Every nation, in every region, now has a decision to make. Either you are with us, or you are with the terrorists. From this day forward, any nation that continues to harbor or support terrorism will be regarded by the United States as a hostile regime.

Our nation has been put on notice: We're not immune from attack. We will take defensive measures against terrorism to protect Americans. Today, dozens of federal departments and agencies, as well as state and local governments, have responsibilities affecting homeland security. These efforts must be coordinated at the highest level. So tonight I announce the creation of a Cabinet-level position reporting directly to me -- the Office of Homeland Security. And tonight I also announce a distinguished

American to lead this effort, to strengthen American security: a military veteran, an effective governor, a true patriot, a trusted friend -- Pennsylvania's Tom Ridge. He will lead, oversee, and coordinate a comprehensive national strategy to safeguard our country against terrorism, and respond to any attacks that may come.

These measures are essential. But the only way to defeat terrorism as a threat to our way of life is to stop it, eliminate it, and destroy it where it grows. Many will be involved in this effort, from FBI agents to intelligence operatives to the reservists we have called to active duty. All deserve our thanks, and all have our prayers. And tonight, a few miles from the damaged Pentagon, I have a message for our military: Be ready. I've called the Armed Forces to alert, and there is a reason. The hour is coming when America will act, and you will make us proud. This is not, however, just America's fight. And what is at stake is not just America's freedom. This is the world's fight. This is civilization's fight. This is the fight of all who believe in progress and pluralism, tolerance and freedom.

We ask every nation to join us. We will ask, and we will need, the help of police forces, intelligence services, and banking systems around the world. The United States is grateful that many nations and many international organizations have already responded -- with sympathy and with support. Nations from Latin America, to Asia, to Africa, to Europe, to the Islamic world. Perhaps the NATO Charter reflects best the attitude of the world: An attack on one is an attack on all. The civilized world is rallying to America's side. They understand that if this terror goes unpunished, their own cities, their own citizens may be next. Terror, unanswered, can not only bring down buildings, it can threaten the stability of legitimate governments. And you know what? We're not going to allow it.

Americans are asking: What is expected of us? I ask you to live your lives, and hug your children. I know many citizens have fears tonight, and I ask you to be calm and resolute, even in the face of a continuing threat. I ask you to uphold the values of America, and remember why so many have come here. We are in a fight for our principles, and our first responsibility is to live by them. No one should be singled out for unfair treatment or unkind words because of their ethnic background or religious faith. I ask you to continue to support the victims of this tragedy with your contributions. Those who want to give can go to a central source of information, libertyunites.org, to find the names of groups providing direct help in New York, Pennsylvania, and Virginia.

The thousands of FBI agents who are now at work in this investigation may need your cooperation, and I ask you to give it. I ask for your patience, with the delays and inconveniences that may accompany tighter security; and for your patience in what will be a long struggle. I ask your continued participation and confidence in the American economy. Terrorists attacked a symbol of American prosperity. They did not touch its source. America is successful because of the hard work, and creativity, and enterprise of our people. These were the true strengths of our economy before September 11th, and they are our strengths today. And, finally, please continue praying for the victims of terror and their families, for those in uniform, and for our great country. Prayer has comforted us in sorrow, and will help strengthen us for the journey ahead.

Tonight I thank my fellow Americans for what you have already done and for what you will do. And ladies and gentlemen of the Congress, I thank you, their representatives, for what you have already done and for what we will do together. Tonight, we face new and sudden national challenges. We will come together to improve air safety, to dramatically expand the number of air marshals on domestic flights, and take new measures to prevent hijacking. We will come together to promote stability and keep our airlines flying, with direct assistance during this emergency. We will come together to give law enforcement the additional tools it needs to track down terror here at home. We will come together to strengthen our intelligence capabilities to know the plans of terrorists before they act, and to find them before they strike.

We will come together to take active steps that strengthen America's economy, and put our people back to work. Tonight we welcome two leaders who embody the extraordinary spirit of all New Yorkers: Governor George Pataki, and Mayor Rudolph Giuliani. As a symbol of America's resolve, my administration will work with Congress, and these two leaders, to show the world that we will rebuild New York City.

After all that has just passed -- all the lives taken, and all the possibilities and hopes that died with them -- it is natural to wonder if America's future is one of fear. Some speak of an age of terror. I know there are struggles ahead, and dangers to face. But this country will define our times, not be defined by them. As long as the United States of America is determined and strong, this will not be an age of terror; this will be an age of liberty, here and across the world.

Great harm has been done to us. We have suffered great loss. And in our grief and anger we have found our mission and our moment. Freedom and fear are at war. The advance of human freedom -- the great achievement of our time, and the great hope of every time -- now depends on us. Our nation, this generation will lift a dark threat of violence from our people and our future. We will rally the world to this cause by our efforts, by our courage. We will not tire, we will not falter, and we will not fail.

It is my hope that in the months and years ahead, life will return almost to normal. We'll go back to our lives and routines, and that is good. Even grief recedes with time and grace. But our resolve must not pass. Each of us will remember what happened that day, and to whom it happened. We'll remember the moment the news came -- where we were and what we were doing. Some will remember an image of a fire, or a story of rescue. Some will carry memories of a face and a voice gone forever.

And I will carry this: It is the police shield of a man named George Howard, who died at the World Trade Center trying to save others. It was given to me by his mom, Arlene, as a proud memorial to her son. This is my reminder of lives that ended, and a task that does not end. I will not forget this wound to our country or those who inflicted it. I will not yield; I will not rest; I will not relent in waging this struggle for freedom and security for the American people. The course of this conflict is not known, yet its outcome is certain. Freedom and fear, justice and cruelty, have always been at war, and we know that God is not neutral between them.

Fellow citizens, we'll meet violence with patient justice -- assured of the rightness of our cause, and confident of the victories to come. In all that lies before us, may God grant us wisdom, and may He watch over the United States of America. Thank you.

 # Sample Speeches

Here are several links to speech outlines. If you've been procrastinating and haven't completed your outline yet AND practiced it, don't delay any longer. You need this time for the information to become second nature to you. These speeches will help you fine tune (or begin) your own speech.

OUTLINES OF SAMPLE SPEECHES

Sample Persuasive Speech "Organ Donation"
http://www.roch.edu/people/lhalverson/sample_persuasive_speech_outline.htm

Sample Demonstrative Speech "Proper Steps in Brushing Teeth"
http://www.ontarioteacher.org/7languagearts/index_htm_files/Demonstration%20Speech%20Sample%20Outline.pdf

Sample Demonstrative Speech "How to Tie a Tie"
http://www.speech-guru.com/sample_demonstration_speech.php

Sample Persuasive Speech "Why We All Need Exercise"
http://department.monm.edu/cata/mcgaan/classes/cata101/Tw-otl.fsc.htm

Sample Informative Speech "Candlemaking"
http://www.roch.edu/people/lhalverson/sample_outline.htm

Speeches

It is important for you to have listened to or read several speeches. This will help you get ideas for anecdotes, transitions, topics and more. Here are several links that will provide you with a large assortment of topics to help prepare you for your DANTES test.

POLITICAL SPEECHES

http://www.americanrhetoric.com/speechbank.htm

http://www.historyplace.com/speeches/previous.htm

http://www.hpol.org/

MOVIE SPEECHES

http://www.americanrhetoric.com/moviespeeches.htm

QUOTATIONS

http://creativequotations.com/

WOMEN LAUREATES SPEECHES

http://gos.sbc.edu/nobel.html

TOP 100 SPEECHES OF ALL TIME

http://gos.sbc.edu/top100.html

How Your Speech is Graded

Your instructor will have a rubric (grade sheet) in which you will get points for the following areas:

Introduction
Was your introduction effective? Did it tie in? Did it grab attention?

Content
Was the content organized? Did it flow? Was there enough research?

Voice Quality
Could you hear and understand the speaker? Was the pitch, pace and annunciation well done?

Non-verbal communication
Did the speaker have tics, swaying or use appropriate gestures?

Eye-Contact
Did the speaker make appropriate eye contact with the audience?

Visual Aids
Did the speaker's visual aids help or hinder the presentation? Were they professional and well done?

Conclusion
Was the conclusion well done? What style of closing did they do (story, restating main points or quotation)?

Because your speech will be completed via audiotape, visual aids and eye-contact won't apply to your speech. However, it is best to act as it the tape recorder is an actual person. Also, for your own benefit, you should take the suggestions of public speaking seriously to improve yourself. Annunciation, pitch, pace and the organization of your speech will be the most important parts of your grade. Make sure you practice sufficiently in front of the mirror, and family and friends to ensure that you are ready and to build your confidence.

This test is given in two parts. The first part is a 84 question multiple choice test. The second portion of the test is your speech. You must pass both portions of test, multiple choice questions and speech in order to get credit for this examination. Your speech must be an impromptu persuasive four minute speech. You will have 10 minutes to prepare to give the speech on a topic that will be given to you on the test day.

There are several reasons for automatic failure on the speech:

Time (If your speech is longer than five minutes or shorter than three minutes you will automatically fail.)

Editing

Not addressing the topic

Not taking a position on the topic

Taking more than one position on the topic

A college professor that teaches Public Speaking will be grading your speech. Sometimes they will be from your same university. You will be graded on the following:

Structure 25%
Delivery 25%
Content/Supporting Information 20%
Effective/Persuasion Level 20%
Language/Style 10%

If you do not pass the speaking portion of the test, you will have to retake the entire test. However, if you feel that you did well, you can pay an additional fee to have your speech re-graded. Some students have reported that having their speech regraded resulted in a passing score. On your score report, it can detail information from the instructor with comments such as: support for the ideas of the speech was inadequate, lacked credibility, or was not relevant to the topic.

 # Vocabulary

Abstract: A summary of an article which was not written by the author of the article.

Abstract words: Words which refer to concepts or ideas.

Acceptance speech: A speech which is given in response to a speech of presentation.

Ad hominem: A fallacy in which a person or speaker is attacked, instead of the related issue.

Adrenaline: A chemical which is released into a person's bloodstream when they become physically or mentally stressed.

After-dinner speech: A thoughtful and lighthearted speech which is meant to entertain.

Alliteration: Repetition of the same sound in close proximity.

Analogical reasoning: An inference method which considers two similar situations and draws conclusions based on the similarity.

Antithesis: Placing an idea and it's acknowledged opposite in close proximity.

Appreciative listening: When a person elects to listen to something for enjoyment.

Atlas: A reference work which displays a collection of maps.

Attitude: A person's opinion about a topic, person, policy or belief.

Audience-centeredness: Preparing and presenting with the audience, and their frame of reference, in mind.

Bandwagon: A fallacy in which it is believed that something which is popular is inherently correct.

Bar graph: A graph which displays data in bars to make comparison easier.

Bibliography: A list of the sources used in a speech.

Bill of Rights: The first 10 amendments to the United States Constitution.

Biographical aid: A reference work with specific focus on a specific person or group.

Brainstorming: Generating ideas by spontaneously sharing ideas or words which come to mind.

Brief example: A specific case briefly mentioned to further explain a concept.

Burden of proof: It is the speaker's job to convince the audience to alter their viewpoint by proving that a policy is necessary.

Call number: A number used in organization and classification of books in a library.

Causal order: When a speech is presented in a cause/effect order.

Causal reasoning: Reasoning with the purpose of determining cause and effect relationships.

Central idea: The thesis of a speech, or a statement which explains the ideas in the speech.

Channel: The means used to communicate a message.

Chart: A table which summarizes or lists large amounts of information.

Chronological order: When a speech is organized with the main points following a time pattern.

Cliché: An overused expression or example.

Clutter: Words which are extra or unnecessary in a speech.

Commemorative speech: A speech which is designed to commemorate or pay tribute to a person, event, group or idea.

Comparative advantages order: A persuasive speech organized so that each main point explains why the speaker's solution is more advantageous than other solutions.

Comparison: A statement which describes similarities between two or more things.

Comprehensive listening: Listening in an effort to understand what the speaker is saying.

Concept: A belief, theory, idea, or principle in an abstract or general form.

Concrete words: Words which refer to specific, tangible things.

Connective: Words or phrases used to relate one idea to the next idea, and create a bridge between the two.

Connotative meaning: The implied or intended meaning of a word or phrase.

Consensus: A state in which all members of the group are in agreement.

Contrast: A statement which describes dissimilarities between two or more things.

Conversational quality: Giving a speech, which has been rehearsed, and making it sound spontaneous.

Creating common ground: A technique in which a speaker creates credibility for themselves by connecting with or relating to the audience.

Credibility: The level to which the audience believes the speaker is qualified to speak about their topic.

Crescendo ending: When a speech builds up to a powerful conclusion.

Criteria: A standard from which comparisons can be drawn, or judgments made.

Critical listening: Listening for the purpose of evaluating and forming an opinion about the message.

Critical thinking: Thinking about things in a focused and logical way, incorporating elements such as relationships, evidence and facts.

Delivery cues: Directions in the speaking outline which remind the speaker how they intended to deliver the speech.

Demographic audience analysis: Analyzing an audience based on location, gender, cultural background, ethnicity, or other demographic factors.

Denotative meaning: The literal dictionary definition of a word or phrase.

Derived credibility: The audience's perception of the speaker's credibility as they are speaking.

Designated leader: A person in a group who is formally appointed or elected to be the leader.

Dialect: The phenomenon in which different locations speak the same language, but with different accents or grammatical patterns.

Direct quotation: Quoting testimony word for word.

Dissolve ending: A conclusion with emotional appeal which diminishes in power, leading to a dramatic final statement.

Dyad: A group which consists of only two people.

Egocentrism: The human tendency to consider a person's own beliefs and values above those of others.

Either-or: A fallacy in which the speaker claims or leads the listeners to believe that there are only two options available, when in fact more exist.

Emergent leader: A person in a group who becomes the leader while the group is convened.

Empathic listening: When a person listens to something in order to support or help the speaker.

Ethical decisions: A decision which involves an ethical question, and must be considered in terms of possible actions weighed against moral guidelines.

Ethics: A branch of philosophy in which the focus is on issues of morality.

Ethnocentrism: When a person believes that their culture is superior to all other cultures.

Ethos: Credibility.

Example: A representative case used to further explain or support a claim.

Expert testimony: Testimony from a person who is a recognized expert about the subject in question.

Extemporaneous speech: Speeches for which preparation has been done, and which are presented with reference to a set of notes.

Extended example: A specific case explained at length to clarify or support a point.

Fallacy: Mistaken, flawed, or incorrect reasoning.

False cause: Mistakenly identifying a cause and effect relationship by assuming that because one event followed another it must have been caused by it.

Feedback: Communication from the listener to the speaker which is generally non-verbal.

Fixed-alternative questions: Questions in which the response is limited to two or more specified alternatives.

Font: A specific style of lettering on a computer.

Frame of reference: A combination of a person's knowledge, goals, values, and experiences which affects how they interpret a message.

Gazetteer: A reference work containing information about geographical topics.

General purpose: The basic goal of a speech, such as to inform, entertain, or persuade.

Gestures: The movements of a speaker's arms or hands during a speech.

Goodwill: Whether to audience believes the speaker has their interests in mind.

Graph: A visual aid which displays numerical data.

Hasty generalization: A fallacy in which a speaker comes to a conclusion based on insufficient or generalized information.

Hearing: When a vibration of sound waves reaches the ear drum, which the brain interprets as sound.

Hidden agenda: Goals of individual members of the group.

Hypothetical Example: An example which uses a generalized or fictitious situation.

Imagery: Words used to create vivid mental pictures.

Implied leader: A person in a group who all the members defer to due to natural characteristics or qualifications.

Impromptu speech: Speeches for which little or no preparation has been done.

Incremental plagiarism: Incorporating an idea from another source and failing to give credit to the source.

Inflections: Changes in a speaker's pitch or tone.

Informative speech: A speech which has the purpose of informing a person about a subject.

Initial credibility: The audience's perception of the speaker's credibility before they speak.

Interference: Something which impedes the communication of a message.

Internal preview: Statements which indicate what the next topic or idea will be in a speech.

Internal summary: A statement summarizing the preceding points of a speech.

Jargon: Technical language which is related to a specific profession or trade.

Key-word outline: A note form which concisely outlines the speaker's main points and evidences.

Kinesics: The study of body language, or how body motions influence and take part in communication.

Leadership: A quality characterized by the ability to influence others to make a group more effective or efficient.

Line graph: A graph in which lines are used to illustrate the changes in a variable over time.

Listener: The person that the speaker is attempting to communicate their message to.

Listening: When a person pays attention to and attempts to understand and interpret what they hear.

Logos: The logic of a speech, which includes the presence of supporting evidence and the strength of the reasoning.

Main points: The concepts, claims or ideas which the speaker will focus on the most.

Maintenance needs: Needs relating to the interpersonal relations between group members.

Manuscript speech: Speeches which are written and delivered word for word.

Mean: The "average" value of a set of numbers, determined by dividing the sum of the terms by the number of terms.

Median: The number which falls at the center of a group of data when organized numerically.

Message: What a speaker is trying to communicate to their listener.

Metaphor: A comparison which does not use the words like or as.

Mixed metaphor: An illogical and confusing metaphor.

Mode: The number which appears the greatest amount of times in a data set.

Monotone: When a speaker's pitch and tone remain constant throughout the speech.

Monroe's motivated sequence: A process which includes attention, need, satisfaction, visualization, and action to persuade a listener.

Multimedia presentation: A presentation which combines two or more types of visual aids.

Name-calling: Words used with the intent of degrading or demeaning a group or person.

Newspaper index: An index which lists specific articles from a collection of newspapers.

Nonverbal communication: Communication which occurs not due to verbalization, but through gestures, facial expressions, or posture.

Online catalogue: A system which tracks all the books in a library by listing them electronically.

Open-ended questions: Questions in which the response is not limited and the person responding can answer however they wish.

Panel discussion: When a moderator presents a topic to a group, or panel, and allows for discussion, occasionally asking questions. Panel discussions take place in front of an audience.

Parallelism: Similar arrangement or structure of words, phrases or sentences which creates an organized pattern.

Paraphrase: A summary or restating of another person's ideas or work.

Patchwork plagiarism: Combining ideas from two or three sources and presenting them as one's own.

Pathos: The emotional appeal of a speech.

Pause: A momentary break in the speech, generally between ideas or thoughts.

Peer testimony: Testimony from a regular person who has had experience with the subject in question.

Periodical index: An index which lists specific articles from a collection of journals or periodicals.

Persuasive speech: A speech in which the purpose is to convince the audience to believe or think a certain way.

Personalize: Making a speech applicable to the individuals in an audience.

Pie graph: A graph used to illustrate the distribution of variables in relation to a whole.

Pitch: How high or low a speaker's voice is.

Plagiarism: Presenting another person's ideas as one's own without their knowledge and consent.

Plan: The speaker's idea for how a stated problem can be solved.

Positive nervousness: A type of nervousness which energizes or motivates a speaker.

Practicality: The feasibility and logic of a speaker's plan.

Preliminary bibliography: A list of books or works which seem like they will have useful information about the topic a speaker is researching.

Preparation outline: A detailed outline including the title, purpose, ideas, main points, subpoints, and conclusion of a speech.

Preview statement: A statement in the beginning of the speech which outlines the main points the speech will focus on.

Problem-cause-solution order: When a speech is organized with the problem stated first, the cause stated second, and the proposed solution stated last.

Problem-solution order: A speech which is organized with a problem presented first, and a solution presented second.

Problem-solving small group: A group of three to twelve people formed to find a solution for a problem.

Procedural needs: The details of the conduct of a group, including location, agenda, and logistical issues.

Process: A system or series of actions which produce a result.

Pronunciation: The accepted way to say a word, including the sound and rhythm of the word.

Question of fact: Question addressing whether or not a statement or assertion is true.

Question of policy: Questions involving the morality or logic of past actions.

Question of value: Questions which address the morality of a concept or idea.

Quoting out of context: Distorting the meaning of a quote by neglecting to explain the situation in which it was presented.

Rate: How quickly or slowly a person speaks.

Reasoning: Using evidence and data to draw conclusions.

Reasoning from principle: Using general principles to come to a conclusion.

Reasoning from specific instances: Using specific facts to come to a conclusion.

Red herring: Diverting attention by introducing an irrelevant issue.

Reference work: A work which summarizes and combines large amounts of information about a subject area.

Repetition: Repeatedly stating the same phrase, word, or idea.

Research interview: An interview with the purpose of gathering information for a speech.

Residual message: The elements from their speech which a speaker wants the listeners to remember.

Rhetorical question: A question which is designed to make the listeners think about the concept, but which is not meant to be answered vocally.

Rhythm: An effect created by arranging words so as to create a pattern in the sounds and stresses of syllables.

Scale questions: Questions in which the response requires specifying a certain level on an interval or scale.

Search engine: A search aid used by researches which finds web pages matching the searchers request.

Sexist language: Language consistent with gender stereotyping.

Signpost: A statement which brings attention to an important concept or idea.

Simile: A comparison which uses the words like or as.

Situation: The combination of location and time at which communication occurs.

Situational audience analysis: Analyzing an audience in terms of setting, occasion, and the audience's prior knowledge or opinions about the subject matter.

Slippery slope: A fallacy which claims that one action will inevitably cause a series of actions.

Small group: A group which consists of between three and twelve people.

Spatial order: When the main points of a speech are presented in a directional pattern.

Speaker: A person who presents an oral message to a listener.

Speaking outline: A brief outline which is used as notes during a speech.

Specific purpose: The exact purpose for which the speaker is giving their speech.

Speech of introduction: A speech which introduces another person, generally the main speaker who the audience came to see.

Speech of presentation: A speech which publicly presents an award or gift to another person.

Speech to gain immediate action: A speech for which the purpose is to persuade an audience to take action in support of a policy.

Speech to gain passive agreement: A speech for which the purpose is to persuade an audience to agree with or support a policy.

Sponsoring organization: The organization which is responsible for the information on a web page.

Stage fright: When a person feels anxious because they have to speak in front of an audience.

Statistic: A numerical figure used to describe a set of data.

Stereotype: The acknowledged traditional belief or oversimplification of an idea, concept or image.

Strategic organization: Preparing a speech with the desired result and intended audience in mind.

Supporting materials: Materials or information which support a speaker's claim.

Symposium: A gathering in which many people present about the same topic.

Target audience: The group or portion of the audience which the speaker most wants to appeal to or persuade.

Task needs: Needs related to the ability of a group to complete their task.

Terminal credibility: The audience's perception of the speaker's credibility after they are finished speaking.

Testimony: Quotations used as supporting evidence.

Thesaurus: A book which lists synonyms of words.

Topic: The subject, theme or category of interest in a speech.

Topical order: When a speech is organized into topics and subtopics, which are presented in logical order.

Transition: Words or phrases used to indicate when a speaker moves to a new idea.

URL: Uniform Resource Locator. The website address.

Virtual library: A search aid which organizes and operates like a traditional library.

Visual framework: A pattern followed in outlining a speech which emphasizes the relations between the elements of the speech.

Visualization: When, in preparation, a speaker imagines themselves giving their presentation successfully.

Vocal variety: A method of making a speech expressive by using inflections and changes in rate.

Vocalized pause: When the speaker fills a pause with "uh" or another vocalization.

Volume: How loud or quiet a speaker is.

Yearbook: A reference work with specific focus on events from the previous year.

Sample Test Questions

1) Which type of connective is the following phrase "now that we have talked about the dangers of smoking, I will talk about the other four contributors to poor health"?

   A) Transition
   B) Internal preview
   C) Internal summary
   D) Signpost

The correct answer is B:) Internal preview. An internal preview reviews what was just covered and introduces the next section.

2) When an audience believes the speaker has credibility before he begins speaking it is called

   A) Initial credibility
   B) Derived credibility
   C) Terminal credibility
   D) Outstanding credibility

The correct answer is A:) Initial credibility. When the speaker already has the audience believing in his credibility it is called initial credibility.

3) A student has to write an essay and doesn't have time to finish it properly. They decide to find a similar essay on the internet and copy some of the paragraphs and ideas into their own essay. This is

   A) Appreciative plagiarism
   B) Global plagiarism
   C) Patchwork plagiarism
   D) Incremental plagiarism

The correct answer is D:) Incremental plagiarism. Incremental plagiarism is incorporating an idea from another source and failing to give credit to the source.

4) The elements of a speech which the speaker wants the audience to remember are called the

    A) Main points
    B) Sub points
    C) Residual message
    D) General purpose

The correct answer is C:) Residual message. The main points, sub points, and general purpose may be part of the residual message, but the question actually defines residual message.

5) An error in reasoning is called

    A) Fallacy
    B) Analogy
    C) Ethos
    D) Simple start

The correct answer is A:) Fallacy.

6) When the audience believes that the speaker has their interests in mind it is called

    A) Credibility
    B) Comrade
    C) Authority
    D) Goodwill

The correct answer is D:) Goodwill.

7) A debater is told to listen to a speech and then write an essay about their opinion of the topic. They are using

    A) Comprehensive listening
    B) Appreciative listening
    C) Critical listening
    D) Empathic listening

The correct answer is C:) Critical listening. Critical listening involves forming an opinion based on what was said.

8) A key-word outline is

    A) When a person pays attention to and attempts to understand and interpret- what they hear.
    B) A note form which concisely outlines the speaker's main points and evidences.
    C) A summary of an article which was not written by the author or the article.
    D) The subject, theme or category of interest in a speech.

The correct answer is B:) A note form which concisely outlines the speaker's main points and evidences.

9) The tendency to consider one's own beliefs and opinions before those of others is called

    A) Attitude
    B) Ethnocentrism
    C) Selfishness
    D) Egocentrism

The correct answer is D:) Egocentrism.

10) Which pattern of organization would be most suitable for the following speech "The History of Coin Collecting"?

    A) Chronological order
    B) Spatial order
    C) Causal order
    D) Problem/solution order

The correct answer is A:) Chronological order.

11) "How many miles is it from my house to campus?" is a question of

    A) Fact
    B) Value
    C) Policy
    D) Morality

The correct answer is A:) Fact.

12) Speeches for which little or no preparation has been done.

    A) Extemporaneous speech
    B) Impromptu speech
    C) Informative speech
    D) Manuscript speech

The correct answer is B:) Impromptu speech.

13) Which pattern of organization would be most suitable for the following speech "Constructing the Statue of Liberty"?

    A) Chronological order
    B) Spatial order
    C) Causal order
    D) Problem/solution order

The correct answer is B:) Spatial order.

14) "How many games has our local sports team won this past year?" is a question of

    A) Fact
    B) Value
    C) Policy
    D) Morality

The correct answer is A:) Fact.

15) Inflections are

    A) How high or low the speaker's voice is.
    B) Changes in a speaker's pitch or tone.
    C) How loud or quiet the speaker is.
    D) Changes in the rate at which a speaker talks.

The correct answer is B:) Changes in the speaker's pitch or tone.

16) Monroe's Motivated Sequence is used in speeches which are meant to be

    A) Introductory
    B) Personal
    C) Entertaining
    D) Persuasive

The correct answer is D:) Persuasive.

17) During a vocalized pause you would not expect to hear

    A) Um
    B) Uh
    C) Er
    D) Therefore

The correct answer D:) Therefore. A vocalized pause is when the speaker fills a pause with "uh," "um," or another vocalization. Therefore would indicate that a speech is moving forward, not a pause.

18) Which of the following is a delivery cue?

    A) Slow down
    B) Speak louder
    C) Display image
    D) All of the above

The correct answer is D:) All of the above. Delivery cues are directions in the speaking outline which remind the speaker how they intended to deliver the speech. All of the answers are delivery cues.

19) A speech which is delivered word for word from a written copy is a(n)

    A) Abstract speech
    B) Informative speech
    C) Manuscript speech
    D) Persuasive speech

The correct answer is C:) Manuscript speech.

20) "How many hours does the average teenager watch television?" is a question of

    A) Fact
    B) Value
    C) Policy
    D) Morality

The correct answer is A:) Fact.

21) "Should teachers be given a raise?" is a question of

    A) Fact
    B) Value
    C) Policy
    D) Morality

The correct answer is C:) Policy.

22) Which pattern of organization would be most suitable for the following speech "The Effects of Cigarettes on the Lungs"?

    A) Chronological order
    B) Spatial order
    C) Causal order
    D) Problem/solution order

The correct answer is C:) Causal order.

23) Multiple choice questions are

    A) Fixed-alternative questions
    B) Open-ended questions
    C) Categorical questions
    D) Scale questions

The correct answer is A:) Fixed-alternative questions. Fixed-alternative questions have specific choices for answers, which is what multiple choice questions do.

24) When you restate someone's words it is called

    A) Quotation
    B) Paraphrase
    C) Testimony
    D) Public speaking

The correct answer is B:) Paraphrase.

25) Changes in the speaker's tone is known as

    A) Pitch
    B) Volume
    C) Inflection
    D) Monotone

The correct answer is C:) Inflection. Inflection is the natural change in the speaker's tone when speaking.

26) Which of the following would NOT be included in a preparation outline?

    A) Title
    B) Purpose
    C) Main points
    D) All of the above would be included

The correct answer is D:) All of the above would be included. A preparation outline is detailed and includes all of the elements listed, along with the ideas and conclusion.

27) In Maslow's hierarchy of needs if you are in the fifth stage you are experiencing which need?

    A) Safety
    B) Food
    C) Respect from others
    D) Realized full potential

The correct answer is D:) Realized full potential.

28) "Should we institute online voting?" is a question of

 A) Fact
 B) Value
 C) Policy
 D) Morality

The correct answer is C:) Policy.

29) Which pattern of organization would be most suitable for the following speech "In Order for Teenagers to Listen, their Parents Must Become Involved"?

 A) Chronological order
 B) Spatial order
 C) Causal order
 D) Problem/solution order

The correct answer is D:) Problem/solution order.

30) Which pattern of organization would be most suitable for the following speech "How to Bake a Cake"?

 A) Chronological order
 B) Spatial order
 C) Causal order
 D) Problem/solution order

The correct answer is A:) Chronological order. Chronological order is starting at a specific period of time (such as the beginning) and following it through step-by-step.

31) A search aid which operates and organizes like a traditional library is a(n)

 A) Online catalogue
 B) Periodical index
 C) Card catalogue
 D) Virtual library

The correct answer is D:) Virtual library.

32) The sum of the data divided by the number of data is called the

    A) Mean
    B) Median
    C) Mode
    D) Mean or Median

The correct answer is A:) Mean.

33) Which pattern of organization would be most suitable for the following speech "How to Keep Off Unwanted Pounds"?

    A) Chronological order
    B) Spatial order
    C) Causal order
    D) Problem/solution order

The correct answer is C:) Causal order.

34) What is NOT an example of plagiarism?

    A) Using someone else's work as your own
    B) Patching together a speech three different pieces of material found online
    C) Telling a foul joke
    D) Paraphrasing a quote

The correct answer is C:) Telling a foul joke. All other answers, A, B and D are examples of plagiarism.

35) A biology teacher is giving a lecture and quotes a famous scientist who works in a genetic laboratory. This is called

    A) Expert testimony
    B) Peer testimony
    C) Quoting out of context
    D) Strategic organization

The correct answer is A:) Expert testimony. Expert testimony is quoting a person who is a recognized expert, as the biology teacher did.

36) Which pattern of organization would be most suitable for the following speech "Constructing a Suspension Bridge"?

    A) Chronological order
    B) Spatial order
    C) Causal order
    D) Problem/solution order

The correct answer is B:) Spatial order.

37) A speech which has the purpose of informing a person about a subject

    A) Extemporaneous speech
    B) Impromptu speech
    C) Informative speech
    D) Manuscript speech

The correct answer is C:) Informative speech.

38) Which pattern of organization would be most suitable for the following speech "The Major Steps in Learning the Piano"?

    A) Chronological order
    B) Spatial order
    C) Causal order
    D) Problem/solution order

The correct answer is A:) Chronological order.

39) Aristotle wrote of which of the following:

    A) Artistic proof
    B) Inartistic proof
    C) Arlenic proof
    D) Artistic proof and inartistic proof

The correct answer is D:) Artistic proof and inartistic proof.

40) Which of the following is NOT an artistic proof?

    A) Ethos
    B) Logos
    C) Pathos
    D) Lobos

The correct answer is D:) Lobos.

41) Which of the following is the second phase of the listening process?

    A) Remembering
    B) Sensing
    C) Understanding
    D) Attending

The correct answer is D:) Attending.

42) Which of the following words are NOT the same as topic?

    A) Theme
    B) Subject
    C) Category
    D) All of the above are the same as topic

The correct answer is D:) All of the above are the same as topic.

43) A search aid can be used to find information

    A) In the library
    B) On the internet
    C) At a person's house
    D) Both A and B

The correct answer is B:) On the internet.

44) Speeches which are written and delivered word for word are called

   A) Extemporaneous speech
   B) Impromptu speech
   C) Informative speech
   D) Manuscript speech

The correct answer is D:) Manuscript speech.

45) Which of the following is NOT a demographic?

   A) Wealth
   B) Attractiveness
   C) Occupation
   D) Education level

The correct answer is B:) Attractiveness.

46) What is the difference between an internal preview and a preview statement?

   A) A preview statement summarizes a speech or article and is written by someone other than the author, and an internal preview is a summary of the speech or article and is written by the author.
   B) An internal preview is at the beginning of a speech and introduces the main points of the speech, and a preview statement is during the essay and summarizes the previous points.
   C) An internal preview is in the middle of a speech and summarizes both the points already stated, and introduces the points coming up, and a preview statement is at the beginning and summarizes all the points which will be in the speech.
   D) A preview statement is at the beginning of a speech and introduces the main points of the speech, and an internal preview is during the essay and summarizes the previous points.

The correct answer is D:) A preview statement is at the beginning of a speech and introduces the main points of the speech, and an internal preview is during the essay and summarizes the previous points.

47) An astronomy teacher is giving a lecture about the solar system. First they talk about the sun, and then all of the planets in order of how close they are to the sun. What is this type of organization called?

   A) Chronological order
   B) Causal order
   C) Topical order
   D) Spatial order

The correct answer is D:) Spatial order. Spatial order is an organization pattern which follows a direction. In this case, the direction is outward from the sun.

48) In Maslow's hierarchy of needs if you are in the second stage you are experiencing which need?

   A) Safety
   B) Food
   C) Respect from others
   D) Realized full potential

The correct answer is A:) Safety.

49) Dialect is

   A) Technical language which is related to a specific profession or trade.
   B) The phenomenon in which different locations speak the same language, but with different accents or grammatical patterns.
   C) The movements of a speaker's arms or hands during a speech.
   D) The study of body language, or how body motions influence and take part in communication.

The correct answer is B:) The phenomenon in which different locations speak the same language, but with different accents or grammatical patterns.

50) When a person feels anxious because they have to speak in front of an audience it is called

   A) Adrenaline
   B) Positive nervousness
   C) Stage fright
   D) Negative nervousness

The correct answer is C:) Stage fright.

51) Which of the following is NOT a step of Monroe's Motivated Sequence?

    A) Attention
    B) Need
    C) Visualization
    D) Rebuttal

The correct answer is D:) Rebuttal. Monroe's Motivated Sequence does not involve rebuttal.

52) The implied or intended meaning of a word or phrase is called

    A) Connotative meaning
    B) Simile
    C) Dialect
    D) Signpost

The correct answer is A:) Connotative meaning.

53) Which of the following refers to credibility?

    A) Ethos
    B) Logos
    C) Pathos
    D) Lobos

The correct answer is A:) Ethos.

54) A speech for which little or no preparation has been done is called a(n)

    A) Informative speech
    B) Impromptu speech
    C) Manuscript speech
    D) After-dinner speech

The correct answer is B:) Impromptu speech.

55) If a speaker wanted to change the word in their speech to a different word with a similar meaning, what would they use?

A) Bibliography
B) Dictionary
C) Concrete words
D) Thesaurus

The correct answer is D:) Thesaurus. A thesaurus lists synonyms, which is what the speaker needs.

56) The phrase "as cold as ice" is a(n)

A) Connotative meaning
B) Concrete word
C) Simile
D) Metaphor

The correct answer is C:) Simile. A simile is a comparison which uses the word like or as.

57) A speaker who repeatedly uses the words "like" and "um" will likely be criticized for

A) Imagery
B) Clichés
C) Rhythm
D) Clutter

The correct answer is D:) Clutter. Clutter is words which are used unnecessarily.

58) A speech with vocal variety will have

    I. Inflections
    II. Changes in volume
    II. Repetition

    A) I only
    B) I and II only
    C) I and III only
    D) II and III only

The correct answer is B:) I and II only. Vocal variety involves changes in rate, volume, pitch and tone of a speech. Repetition can be used in a speech, but it is not related to vocal variety.

59) How many types of visual aids are in a multimedia presentation?

    A) One only
    B) Two only
    C) Three only
    D) Two or more

The correct answer is D:) Two or more.

60) What is the difference between denotation and connotation?

    A) Denotation is the literal meaning of a word and connotation is the implied meaning of a word.
    B) Connotation is the literal meaning of a word and denotation is the implied meaning of a word.
    C) Denotation is a lowering of pitch and connotation is an elevating of pitch.
    D) Denotation is speaking at a slower rate and connotation is speaking at a faster rate.

The correct answer is A:) Denotation is the literal meaning of a word and connotation is the implied meaning of a word.

61) The first ten amendments to the Constitution are called the

   A) Bill of Rights
   B) Declaration of Independence
   C) Magna Carta
   D) Constitution's conclusion

The correct answer is A:) Bill of Rights.

62) A comparison which uses the words like or as is called

   A) Connotative meaning
   B) Simile
   C) Dialect
   D) Signpost

The correct answer is B:) Simile.

63) Ethical decisions must be considered from what standpoint?

   A) Logical
   B) Rational
   C) Scientific
   D) Moral

The correct answer is D:) Moral. Ethics is a branch of philosophy which involves issues of morality.

64) Speeches for which preparation has been done, and which are presented with reference to a set of notes are called

   A) Extemporaneous speech
   B) Impromptu speech
   C) Informative speech
   D) Manuscript speech

The correct answer is A:) Extemporaneous speech.

65) When is the best time to begin research for a speech?

    A) Before you have selected a topic
    B) While narrowing your topics from three to one
    C) As soon as you read a book about it
    D) As soon as possible

The correct answer is D:) As soon as possible. The more time that you give yourself to prepare, the better off you will be.

66) An anecdote is a

    A) Joke
    B) Story
    C) Limerick
    D) Paraphrased quotation

The correct answer is B:) Story.

67) Which type of connective is the following phrase "let's now discuss"?

    A) Transition
    B) Internal preview
    C) Internal summary
    D) Signpost

The correct answer is A:) Transition.

68) Opening lines should NOT be ambiguous because

    A) Ambiguous language is not grammatically correct.
    B) The speaker will lose the audience's attention if they are too interesting.
    C) Primacy dictates that audiences will remember the first thing they heard.
    D) If they are ambiguous it will be more difficult to make a clear and specific conclusion.

The correct answer is C:) Primacy dictates that audiences will remember the first thing they heard. An audience will best remember a viewpoint the first way they heard it, so opening statements should be very clear.

69) Which of the following is NOT a type of persuasive speech?

    A) Question of fact
    B) Question of value
    C) Question of morals
    D) Question of policy

The correct answer is C:) Question of morals.

70) Which of the following is NOT a type of reasoning?

    A) Deductive
    B) Inductive
    C) Analogical
    D) Either/or

The correct answer is D:) Either/or.

71) Which reasoning fallacy is also known as circular reasoning?

    A) Begging the question
    B) Hasty generalization
    C) Slippery slope
    D) Red herring

The correct answer is A:) Begging the question.

72) When giving a speech without a bias it is known as

    A) Partisan
    B) Non-partisan
    C) Causal
    D) Ad populum

The correct answer is B:) Non-partisan.

73) The group or portion of the audience which the speaker most wants to appeal to or persuade is called

    A) Implied leader
    B) Emergent leader
    C) Consensus
    D) Target audience

The correct answer is D:) Target audience.

74) Which type of connective is the following phrase "How can we now better ourselves?"

    A) Transition
    B) Internal preview
    C) Internal summary
    D) Signpost

The correct answer is D:) Signpost.

75) A book of synonyms is known as a

    A) Dictionary
    B) Encyclopedia
    C) Thesaurus
    D) Rhyming dictionary

The correct answer is C:) Thesaurus.

76) The meaning suggested by emotions triggered by a word is known as

    A) Connotative
    B) Denotative
    C) Concrete
    D) Abstract

The correct answer is A:) Connotative.

77) The literal meaning of a phrase is called

    A) Denotative meaning
    B) Connotative meaning
    C) Concrete meaning
    D) Abstract meaning

The correct answer is A:) Denotative meaning.

78) A student forgets that they have to give a speech about the Constitution and quickly copies a speech off of the internet. This is called

    A) Appreciative plagiarism
    B) Global plagiarism
    C) Patchwork plagiarism
    D) Incremental plagiarism

The correct answer is B:) Global plagiarism. Global plagiarism involves using another person's work in its entirety and presenting it as one's own.

79) Reasoning with the purpose of determining cause and effect is called

    A) Reasoning from specific instances
    B) Analogical reasoning
    C) Reasoning from principle
    D) Causal reasoning

The correct answer is D:) Causal reasoning.

80) If a person wished to persuade their audience to do something they would give a

    A) Speech to gain immediate action
    B) Speech of introduction
    C) Speech to gain active agreement
    D) Speech of presentation

The correct answer is A:) Speech to gain immediate action. A speech to gain immediate action is a speech for which the purpose is to persuade an audience to take action in support of a policy.

81) When a speech is carefully prepared it is known as an

    A) Extemporaneous speech
    B) Conversational speech
    C) Impromptu speech
    D) Manuscript speech

The correct answer is A:) Extemporaneous speech.

82) Which of the following refers to the highness or lowness of a speaker's voice?

    A) Pitch
    B) Volume
    C) Inflection
    D) Monotone

The correct answer is A:) Pitch.

83) The constant tone of a speaker's voice is known as

    A) Pitch
    B) Volume
    C) Inflection
    D) Monotone

The correct answer is D:) Monotone.

84) Which of the following is a statistic?

    I. Mean
    II. Median
    III. Mode

    A) I only
    B) I and II only
    C) I and III only
    D) I, II and III

The correct answer is D:) I, II and III. A statistic is a numerical figure which describes data, which means, medians, and modes all do.

85) A person is trying to describe to their friend why they believe that speeding is justified. As an example they say "If someone needs to get to the hospital quickly, they should be able to speed." This is a(n)

  A) Extended example
  B) Statistic
  C) Brief example
  D) Hypothetical example

The correct answer is D:) Hypothetical Example. This is a hypothetical example because it is a generalized case which the person used to prove their point.

86) A speaker knows that their thesis contradicts what most of their audience believes, and they organize their speech so that their evidence is presented before they state their opinion. This is called

  A) Topical order
  B) Strategic organization
  C) Connective
  D) Spatial order

The correct answer is B:) Strategic organization.

87) Which type of connective is the following phrase "we've discussed the main key point behind getting children to stay in school"?

  A) Transition
  B) Internal preview
  C) Internal summary
  D) Signpost

The correct answer is C:) Internal summary.

88) Stephanie is trying to convince her parents to let her have a party, and says "You should let me have a party. My birthday is coming up fast, it's only a week away. All of my friends have had parties for their birthdays. Plus, you let all of the other kids have parties for their birthdays." Which steps of Toulmin's argument model has she not covered?

A) Claim
B) Warrant
C) Backing
D) More than one step has not been covered

The correct answer is D:) More than one step has not been covered. Stephanie has not offered a qualifying statement or rebuttal.

89) A person in a group who becomes the leader while the group is convened is called

A) Implied leader
B) Emergent leader
C) Consensus
D) Target audience

The correct answer is B:) Emergent leader.

90) The loudness of a speaker's voice is known as

A) Pitch
B) Volume
C) Inflection
D) Monotone

The correct answer is B:) Volume.

91) A speaker wishes to display a graph which has the mean income for various countries on it. Which type of graph should they use?

A) Bar graph
B) Line graph
C) Chart
D) Histogram

The correct answer is A:) Bar graph. Bar graphs are used to display data in an easily comparable way.

92) A dentist is asked to give a presentation for an elementary school class about what they do for their job. What type of speech will they be giving?

    A) Informative speech
    B) Speech of introduction
    C) Acceptance speech
    D) Commemorative speech

The correct answer is A:) Informative speech. An informative speech is used to teach about a subject.

93) Kinesics is

    A) A type of anecdote
    B) Transitions
    C) The study of body language
    D) The last part of the outline

The correct answer is C:) The study of body language.

94) "Capital punishment is wrong and violates our laws" is a question of

    A) Fact
    B) Value
    C) Policy
    D) Morality

The correct answer is B:) Value.

95) A person in a group who all the members defer to due to natural characteristics or qualifications is called

    A) Implied leader
    B) Emergent leader
    C) Consensus
    D) Target audience

The correct answer is A:) Implied leader.

96) Which of the following is NOT a step of Toulmin's argumentation model?

A) Claim
B) Evidence
C) Warrant
D) Satisfaction

The correct answer is D:) Satisfaction. Satisfaction is a step of Monroe's Motivated Sequence.

97) A speaker is doing a presentation on the levels of television usage over the past twenty years. Which type of graph should they use?

A) Bar graph
B) Line graph
C) Chart
D) Histogram

The correct answer is B:) Line graph. Line graphs are used to show changes in a variable over time.

98) Which pattern of organization would be most suitable for the following speech "Renewing a Marriage License After Five Years Will Reduce Divorce"?

A) Chronological order
B) Spatial order
C) Causal order
D) Topical order

The correct answer is C:) Causal order.

99) Which of the following is NOT a goal of public speaking?

A) To inform
B) To persuade
C) To plagiarize
D) To entertain

The correct answer is C:) To plagiarize.

100) Technical language which is related to a specific profession is called

  A) Concept
  B) Font
  C) Practicality
  D) Jargon

The correct answer is D:) Jargon.

101) When a speaker attempts to apply their speech to the individuals in an audience, it is called

  A) Consensus
  B) Dyad
  C) Practicality
  D) Personalizing

The correct answer is D:) Personalizing.

102) "Tennis playing is the game of champions" is a question of

  A) Fact
  B) Value
  C) Policy
  D) Morality

The correct answer is B:) Value.

103) A speaker wishes to convince an audience that they should buy a product. They are giving a(n)

  A) Speech of introduction
  B) Informative speech
  C) Persuasive speech
  D) After-dinner speech

The correct answer is C:) Persuasive speech. A persuasive speech is a speech which attempts to convince the audience to believe a certain way. In this case, the speaker wants the audience to believe that they should buy the product.

104) A question which addresses the morality of a concept or idea is a

    A) Question of policy
    B) Question of practicality
    C) Question of false cause
    D) Question of value

The correct answer is D:) Question of value.

105) Which pattern of organization would be most suitable for the following speech "Famous Women Speakers"?

    A) Chronological order
    B) Spatial order
    C) Causal order
    D) Problem/solution order

The correct answer is A:) Chronological order.

106) A gazetteer contains what type of information?

    A) A specific person
    B) Newspaper articles
    C) Maps
    D) Geographical topics

The correct answer is D:) Geographical topics.

107) What is the mean of {2, 3, 4, 8, 8, 10}?

    A) 2
    B) 5.8
    C) 6.7
    D) 8

The correct answer is B:) 5.8.

108) A speaker giving a lecture about the Revolutionary War begins by discussing the events which led up to the war and ends by speaking about the writing of the Constitution. What is the type of organization called?

A) Chronological order
B) Topical order
C) Problem-cause-solution order
D) Spatial order

The correct answer is A:) Chronological order. Chronological order follows a timeline format.

109) How high or low a speaker's voice is called

A) Logos
B) Pitch
C) Ethos
D) Dyad

The correct answer is B:) Pitch.

110) "Is there a need for more student parking on campus?" is a question of

A) Fact
B) Value
C) Policy
D) Morality

The correct answer is C:) Policy.

111) A speaker discusses the topic of whether or not it was right to drop an atomic bomb in Hiroshima during WWII. They are discussing a(n)

A) Question of policy
B) Question of practicality
C) Question of false cause
D) Question of value

The correct answer is A:) Question of policy. Although it may seem like the situation deals with morality (which would make it a question of value) it is not. It was a past action so it is considered to be a question of policy.

112) A person goes to hear the President of a university talk about policies at the university. The person listens to the President because he has

    A) Derived credibility
    B) Initial credibility
    C) Terminal credibility
    D) Inherent credibility

The correct answer is B:) Initial credibility. Before the person has even heard the President, they believe that he is qualified to speak about the subject, giving him initial credibility.

113) Which of the following is NOT an example of nonverbal communication?

    A) Crossing your arms
    B) Posture
    C) Eye contact
    D) Whispering

The correct answer is D:) Whispering.

114) What is it called when someone expresses themselves clearly?

    A) Stuttering
    B) Articulate
    C) Nasality
    D) Coached

The correct answer is B:) Articulate.

115) The literal meaning of a word is called

    A) Connotative
    B) Denotative
    C) Articulate
    D) None of the above

The correct answer is B:) Denotative. A denotative meaning is the literal meaning of a word.

116) A person goes to a speech from a person they have never heard of before. While listening to the speaker, the person realizes that the speaker is very well informed about the issue. The speaker has

A) Derived credibility
B) Initial credibility
C) Terminal credibility
D) Inherent credibility

The correct answer is A:) Derived credibility. They speaker proved himself qualified to speak on the subject during the speech, giving him derived credibility.

117) Which of the following is another word for credibility?

A) Logos
B) Pathos
C) Ethos
D) Dyad

The correct answer is C:) Ethos.

118) When asked if they support the governor's policies for public education, a speaker brings up his disgust toward the governor due to his recent divorce. This is called

A) Bandwagon
B) Slippery slope
C) Either-or
D) Ad hominem

The correct answer is D:) Ad hominem. In an ad hominem, the person is attacked, instead of their policies.

119) A class is instructed to break into groups and choose a leader. This person is the

A) Implied leader
B) Emergent leader
C) Logical leader
D) Designated leader

The correct answer is D:) Designated leader. A designated leader is chosen or elected by the group.

120) Needs relating to interpersonal relations between group members are

    A) Task needs
    B) Maintenance needs
    C) Hidden agendas
    D) Communicative needs

The correct answer is B:) Maintenance needs.

121) A consensus is

    A) When none of the members in a group agree with each other.
    B) When only a small portion of the members in a group agree with each other.
    C) When exactly half of the members in the group agree with each other.
    D) When all of the members of a group agree with each other.

The correct answer is D:) When all of the members of a group agree with each other.

122) The acknowledged traditional belief or oversimplification of an idea, concept or image.

    A) Logical
    B) Pathos
    C) Stereotype
    D) Testimony

The correct answer is C:) Stereotype.

123) Critical thinking is

    A) Logical
    B) Focused
    C) Supported by evidence
    D) All of the above

The correct answer is D:) All of the above. Critical thinking is described by all of the statements.

124) Frame of reference includes a person's

    A) Knowledge
    B) Interests
    C) Goals
    D) All of the above

The correct answer is D:) All of the above. Frame of reference also includes values.

125) When a person believes their culture is superior to all other cultures it is called

    A) Ethnocentrism
    B) Interference
    C) Situation
    D) Plagiarism

The correct answer is A:) Ethnocentrism.

126) A teenager, who loves music, constantly has music playing. This is called

    A) Comprehensive listening
    B) Appreciative listening
    C) Empathic listening
    D) Critical listening

The correct answer is B:) Appreciative listening. Appreciative listening involves listening for enjoyment.

127) When a test consists of an essay, the essay is called an

    A) Fixed-alternative question
    B) Open-ended question
    C) Categorical question
    D) Scale question

The correct answer is B:) Open-ended question. Open-ended questions allow for any type of response.

128) An abstract is

    A) A person's opinion about a topic, person, policy or belief.
    B) A work which summarizes and combines large amounts of information about a subject area.
    C) A note form which concisely outlines the speaker's main points and evidences.
    D) A summary of an article which was not written by the author of the article.

The correct answer is D:) A summary of an article which was not written by the author of the article.

129) An atlas contains what type of information?

    A) A specific person
    B) Newspaper articles
    C) Maps
    D) Information about the previous year

The correct answer is C:) Maps.

130) A statement which summarizes the preceding points in a speech is called a(n)

    A) Internal preview
    B) Signpost
    C) Preparation outline
    D) Internal summary

The correct answer is D:) Internal summary.

131) A bibliography is

    A) A statement summarizing the preceding points of a speech.
    B) A brief outline which is used as notes during a speech.
    C) A list of the sources used in a speech.
    D) Directions in the speaking outline which remind the speaker how they intended to deliver the speech.

The correct answer is C:) A list of the sources used in a speech.

132) What is the suggested meaning of a word based on context?

    A) Connotative
    B) Denotative
    C) Articulate
    D) None of the above

The correct answer is A:) Connotative. The connotative meaning of a word is when you use a word figuratively speaking or use it to evoke emotions linked to a specific word. For example, you might use the word home when describing something that makes you feel happy and comfortable. A student might use this in a speech by saying, "We feel at home in our public speaking class." This is connotative because they do not mean that the students literally live at the school.

133) Using evidence and data to draw conclusions is called

    A) Hasty generalization
    B) Leadership
    C) Reasoning
    D) Symposium

The correct answer is C:) Reasoning.

134) During a debate a speaker is asked about their opinion on war and begins to talk about their goal to lower taxes by decreasing government salaries. This is called a(n)

    A) Bandwagon
    B) Slippery slope
    C) Either-or
    D) Red herring

The correct answer is D:) Red herring. The speaker brings up the taxes, an irrelevant issue, to draw attention away from the subject of war. This is called a red herring.

135) When you are unsure of a word you should

    A) Use it frequently
    B) Divine what it means through conjecture
    C) Look it up in the dictionary
    D) Incorporate it into your speech

The correct answer is C:) Look it up in the dictionary. Never use a word when you are not absolutely sure what it means. This is particularly true when preparing a speech.

136) When your speech uses too many words to say a simple thought it is

    A) Improperly organized
    B) Cluttered
    C) Abstract
    D) Articulate

The correct answer is B:) Cluttered. Being cluttered means using too many words or phrases to say a simple statement or idea. Politicians and other long winded speakers are good examples of cluttered speakers. In a public speaking class, eliminating clutter will result in a much more persuasive speech.

137) When you use the words "like" or "as" in a comparison it is called

    A) An analogy
    B) A metaphor
    C) A cliché
    D) A simile

The correct answer is D:) A simile. A simile is a comparison that uses the words like or as. For example, "She dances as if there is no one else in the room."

138) The statement "it's raining cats and dogs" is

    A) An analogy
    B) A metaphor
    C) A cliché
    D) A simile

The correct answer is C:) A cliché. A cliché is a once unique, now worn out, trivial metaphor. Clichés should be avoided in speech making.

139) Maslow's Hierarchy of Needs consists of the following stages from the top down

    A) Self-actualization, esteem, belonging and love, safety, physical
    B) Physical, safety, belonging and love, esteem, self-actualization
    C) Physical, belonging and love, esteem, safety, self-actualization
    D) Belonging and love, safety, physical, esteem, self-actualization

The correct answer is A:) Self-actualization, esteem, belonging and love, safety, physical. These are the needs from the top of the pyramid down.

140) At a high school assembly, the student body president explains to everybody who their speaker will be, and tells some details about them. This is called a(n)

    A) Persuasive speech
    B) Speech of introduction
    C) Informative speech
    D) Commemorative speech

The correct answer is B:) Speech of introduction. The student body president is introducing the speaker.

141) When you DO NOT use the words "like" or "as" in a comparison it is called

    A) An analogy
    B) A metaphor
    C) A cliché
    D) A simile

The correct answer is B:) A metaphor. A metaphor is a comparison that DOES NOT use the words like or as. For example, "America's workers are the gears of society." This statement makes a comparison but specifically does not use either word, like or as.

142) In Maslow's hierarchy of needs if you are in the third stage you are experiencing which need?

    A) Safety
    B) Food
    C) Respect from others
    D) Love

The correct answer is D:) Love.

143) When you arrange statements that are similar or specific opposites you are using

    A) Alliteration
    B) Stereotype
    C) Parallelism
    D) Antithesis

The correct answer is C:) Parallelism. Parallelism is grouping together statements with similar meanings to get across a point. The statement "by the people and for the people" is an example of parallelism.

144) A person gets a team together for a knowledge competition. Although not an official leader, the person organizes meeting and study schedules for everyone because they have been to the competition before and know how it is structured. They are the

    A) Implied leader
    B) Emergent leader
    C) Logical leader
    D) Designated leader

The correct answer is A:) Implied leader. The other group members listen to this person because they recognize their expertise in the matter, making them an implied leader.

145) A group leader is chosen to determine a meeting place, set up meeting schedules, and create an agenda. The group leader is responsible for

    A) Maintenance needs
    B) Task needs
    C) Procedural needs
    D) Hidden agendas

The correct answer is C:) Procedural needs. All of the listed responsibilities are procedural needs.

146) Contrasting ideas is called

A) Alliteration
B) Stereotype
C) Parallelism
D) Antithesis

The correct answer is D:) Antithesis. Using the exact opposite of your expression can get your point across. The phrase "give me liberty or give me death" is an example of antithesis.

147) "All blondes are dumb" is an example of

A) Alliteration
B) Stereotype
C) Parallelism
D) Antithesis

The correct answer is B:) Stereotype.

148) A company pays for their employees to go to a conference which will have five speakers who all speak about different elements of cutting edge computer techniques. This is most correctly called a(n)

A) Informative speech
B) Panel discussion
C) Themed discussion
D) Symposium

The correct answer is D:) Symposium. While each of the speakers will most likely give an informative speech, when a group gathers to hear multiple speeches about the same topic, it is called a symposium.

149) A person who presents a message to another person or group of people is called a

A) Channel
B) Listener
C) Speaker
D) Message

The correct answer is C:) Speaker.

150) The emotional appeal of a speech is called

    A) Ethos
    B) Bandwagon
    C) Pathos
    D) Dyad

The correct answer is A:) Ethos.

151) Alliteration of the repetition of a sound. Which of the following is an example of alliteration?

    A) Fathers-forth
    B) Beauty is past change
    C) Dappled snow
    D) Brindle cow

The correct answer is A:) Fathers-forth. The repetition of the "f" sound creates the alliteration.

152) A person practices giving a speech to their friends and asks for their opinions about how to make it better. The friends are using

    A) Comprehensive listening
    B) Appreciative listening
    C) Critical listening
    D) Empathic listening

The correct answer is D:) Empathic listening. Empathic listening is for the purpose of supporting or helping the speaker.

153) Demographic audience analysis considers elements such as

    A) Age
    B) Gender
    C) Cultural beliefs
    D) All of the above

The correct answer is D:) All of the above.

154) A question which is not meant to be answered verbally is a(n)

A) Fixed-alternative question
B) Open-ended question
C) Rhetorical question
D) Scale question

The correct answer is C:) Rhetorical question. Rhetorical questions are meant to lead the audience to think about the answer, but not respond vocally.

155) The science of body language is called

A) Dialect
B) Pronunciation
C) Kinesics
D) Monotone

The correct answer is C:) Kinesics. Kinesics is the study of body language in respect to communication.

156) The phenomenon in which different locations speak the same language, but with different accents or grammatical patterns.

A) Connotative meaning
B) Simile
C) Dialect
D) Signpost

The correct answer is C:) Dialect.

157) A teenager begs their parents to let them go see a movie because all of their friends are seeing it. This is called

A) Bandwagon
B) Slippery slope
C) Either-or
D) Ad hominem

The correct answer is A:) Bandwagon. In this fallacy, it is assumed that because something is popular, it must be right.

158) After winning first prize at a talent contest, an individual is expected to give a(n)

   A) Speech of introduction
   B) Commemorative speech
   C) Acceptance speech
   D) Informative speech

The correct answer is C:) Acceptance speech. In an acceptance speech a speaker gives thanks for receiving an award, gift, or another form of public recognition.

159) How many people are in a small group?

   A) 2-4
   B) 5-10
   C) 3-12
   D) 7-10

The correct answer is C:) 3-12.

160) The way a word is spoken

   A) Dialect
   B) Pronunciation
   C) Kinesics
   D) Monotone

The correct answer is B:) Pronunciation.

161) In Maslow's hierarchy of needs if you are in the fourth stage you are experiencing which need?

   A) Safety
   B) Food
   C) Respect from others
   D) Love

The correct answer is C:) Respect from others.

162) Language that is unique based on accent, pronunciation or vocabulary

A) Dialect
B) Articulate
C) Kinesics
D) Monotone

The correct answer is A:) Dialect.

163) Recency refers to the idea that

A) The more recently a law has been proposed, the more negative the opinion about it is.
B) An audience is most likely to remember the concluding statements of a speech.
C) Most audiences will remember a speech only if it convinces them of a need they have.
D) An audience is most likely to remember the opening statements of a speech.

The correct answer is B:) An audience is most likely to remember the concluding statements of a speech. The first thing a listener remembers is often the last thing they heard.

164) A speaker is doing a presentation about the use of fossil fuels and wishes to display a graph which shows what percentage of energy comes from fossil fuels. Which type of graph should they use?

A) Line graph
B) Bar graph
C) Pie graph
D) Chart

The correct answer is C:) Pie graph. Pie graphs are used to show how one variable relates to a whole.

165) In Maslow's hierarchy of needs if you are in the first stage you are experiencing which need?

A) Safety
B) Food
C) Respect from others
D) Love

The correct answer is B:) Food.

166) At a book club meeting, all of the members vote on the next book to be read. The book which receives the most votes will be chosen. All of the books are numbered, and the members write their books down. The president looks at all the numbers. Which of the following measurements is used to determine what the next book will be?

A) Mean
B) Median
C) Mode
D) Range

The correct answer is C:) Mode. The president will determine which book to read based on which number occurs the most, or which book had the most votes, which is the mode.

167) A statement which brings attention to an important concept or idea is called

A) Connotative meaning
B) Simile
C) Dialect
D) Signpost

The correct answer is D:) Signpost.

168) Believing your race is superior to any other is called

A) Racism
B) Ethnocentrism
C) Ego
D) Intelligence model

The correct answer is B:) Ethnocentrism.

169) A student in a classroom listens intently to their teacher's lecture. This is called

A) Comprehensive listening
B) Appreciative listening
C) Empathic listening
D) Critical listening

The correct answer is A:) Comprehensive listening. Comprehensive listening involves trying to understand what is being said.

170) A fallacy in which it is believed that something which is popular is inherently correct is called

A) False cause
B) Bandwagon
C) Cliché
D) Dyad

The correct answer is B:) Bandwagon.

Test Taking Strategies

Here are some test-taking strategies that are specific to this test and to other DSST tests in general:

- Keep your eyes on the time. Pay attention to how much time you have left.

- Read the entire question and read all the answers. Many questions are not as hard to answer as they may seem. Sometimes, a difficult sounding question really only is asking you how to read an accompanying chart. Chart and graph questions are on most DANTES/DSST tests and should be an easy free point.

- If you don't know the answer immediately, the new computer-based testing lets you mark questions and come back to them later if you have time.

- Read the wording carefully. Some words can give you hints to the right answer. There are no exceptions to an answer when there are words in the question such as always, all or none. If one of the answer choices includes most or some of the right answers, but not all, then that is not the answer. Here is an example:

    The primary colors include all of the following:
    A) Red, Yellow, Blue, Green
    B) Red, Green, Yellow
    C) Red, Orange, Yellow
    D) Red, Yellow, Blue

Although item A includes all the right answers, it also includes an incorrect answer, making it incorrect. If you didn't read it carefully, were in a hurry, or didn't know the material well, you might fall for this.

- Make a guess on a question that you do not know the answer to. There is no penalty for an incorrect answer. Eliminate the answer choices that you know are incorrect. For example, this will let your guess be a 1 in 3 chance instead.

What Your Score Means

Based on your score, you may, or may not, qualify for credit at your specific institution. The current ACE recommended score for this exam is 46. Your school may require a higher or lower score to receive credit. To find out what score you need for credit, you need to get that information from your school's website or academic advisor.

You lose no points for incorrect questions so make sure you answer each question. If you don't know, make an educated guess. On this particular test, you must answer 104 questions in 90 minutes.

Test Preparation

How much you need to study depends on your knowledge of a subject area. If you are interested in literature, took it in school, or enjoy reading then your study and preparation for the literature or humanities test will not need to be as intensive as that of someone who is new to literature.

This book is much different than the regular CLEP study guides. This book actually teaches you the information that you need to know to pass the test. If you are particularly interested in an area, or feel that you want more information, do a quick search online. We've tried not to include too much depth in areas that are not as essential on the test. It is important to understand all major theories and concepts listed in the table of contents. It is also important to know any bolded words.

Don't worry if you do not understand or know a lot about the area. With minimal study, you can complete and pass the test.

One of the fallacies of other test books is test questions. People assume that the content of the questions are similar to what will be on the test. That is not the case. They are only there to test your "test taking skills" so for those who know to read a question carefully, there is not much added value from taking a "fake" test. So we have constructed our test questions differently. We will use them to teach you new information not covered in the study guide AND to test your knowledge of items you should already know from reading the text. If you don't know the answer to the test question, review the material. If it is new information, then this is an area that will be covered on the test but not in detail.

To prepare for the test, make a series of goals. Allot a certain amount of time to review the information you have already studied and to learn additional material. Take notes as you study; it will help you learn the material. If you haven't done so already, download the study tips guide from the website and use it to start your study plan.

Legal Note

FLASHCARDS

This section contains flashcards for you to use to further your understanding of the material and test yourself on important concepts, names or dates. Read the term or question then flip the page over to check the answer on the back. Keep in mind that this information may not be covered in the text of the study guide. Take your time to study the flashcards, you will need to know and understand these concepts to pass the test.

Artistic appeal	Ethos
Acceptance speech	**Analogical reasoning**
Logos	**Pathos**
Dialect	**Deductive reasoning**

Type of person that you are and your skills, i.e., education, values, speech delivery skills

Types of appeals that speakers could control such as the way speakers presented their case

An inference method which considers two similar situations and draws conclusions based on the similarity

A speech which is given in response to a speech of presentation

Appeals to the listener's passions, emotions, thoughts and wants

Appeals to the intellect

Using a general conclusion to support a specific argument

The phenomenon in which different locations speak the same language, but with different accents or grammatical patterns

Inductive reasoning

Question of fact

Frame of reference

Causal reasoning

Hasty generalization

Begging the question

Symposium

Target audience

Question addressing whether or not a statement or assertion is true

Using specific cases to support a general conclusion

Implying a link between two items, ideas, etc.

A combination of a person's knowledge, goals, values, and experiences which affects how they interpret a message

Circular reasoning

When you draw a conclusion based on a sample group that is too small

The group or portion of the audience which the speaker most wants to appeal to or persuade

A gathering in which many people present about the same topic

Task needs

"Now that we have talked about the dangers of smoking, I will talk about the other four contributors to poor health"

Fallacy

Topical order

Transition

Font

Goodwill

Pie graph

Internal preview

Needs related to the ability of a group to complete their task

When a speech is organized into topics and subtopics, which are presented in logical order

An error in reasoning

A specific style of lettering on a computer

Words or phrases used to indicate when a speaker moves to a new idea

A graph used to illustrate the distribution of variables in relation to a whole

When the audience believes that the speaker has their interests in mind

Speech to gain passive agreement

Gazetteer

Plagiarism

Ethnocentrism

Anecdote

Parallelism

Paraphrase

Patchwork plagiarism

A reference work containing information about geographical topics

A speech for which the purpose is to persuade an audience to agree with or support a policy

Believing your race is superior to any other

Using someone's work as your own

Similar arrangement or structure of words, phrases or sentences which creates an organized pattern

A story

Combining ideas from two or three sources and presenting them as one's own

A summary or restating of another person's ideas or work

Speaker	Non-partisan
Jargon	Hidden agenda
Hypothetical Example	Connotative
Denotative meaning	Metaphor

Giving a speech without a bias

A person who presents an oral message to a listener

Goals of individual members of the group

Technical language which is related to a specific profession or trade

Meaning suggested by associates or emotions triggered by a word

An example which uses a generalized or fictitious situation

A comparison which does not use the words like or as

Literal meaning or a phrase

Extemporaneous speech	**Pitch**
Monotone	**Kinesics**
Chronological order	**Dyad**
Mean	**Simile**

Highness or lowness of a speaker's voice

When a speech is carefully prepared

Study of body language

Constant tone of a speaker's voice

A group which consists of only two people

Progressing through time, any how-to speech

A comparison which uses the words like or as

The "average" value of a set of numbers, determined by dividing the sum of the terms by the number of terms

Preview statement

Causal order

Median

Key-word outline

Problem/solution order

Internal summaries

Signposts

Testimony

Showing a cause/effect relationship

A statement in the beginning of the speech which outlines the main points the speech will focus on

A note form which concisely outlines the speaker's main points and evidences

The number which falls at the center of a group of data when organized numerically

Reminds listeners of what they just heard

First point shows the problem, the second the solution

Quotations used as supporting evidence

Asking questions, showing where you are in a speech

Inflections

Informative speech

Thesaurus

Line graph

Listener

Question of value

Question of policy

Red herring

A speech which has the purpose of informing a person about a subject

Changes in a speaker's pitch or tone

A graph in which lines are used to illustrate the changes in a variable over time

A book which lists synonyms of words

About the morality, rightness, wrongness, worth

The person that the speaker is attempting to communicate their message to

Where you introduce unrelated information that misdirects attention

Whether or not a specific action should or should not be taken

Non-sequitur

Rhythm

Scale questions

Analogical fallacy

Ad Hominem

Slippery slope

Burden of proof

Spare "brain time"

An effect created by arranging words so as to create a pattern in the sounds and stresses of syllables

When the conclusion does not relate to the proof or evidence

Assuming that two things that are similar are equal

Questions in which the response requires specifying a certain level on an interval or scale

When you assume that when one thing happens, it will create a domino effect

When you attack the person raising an issue, not the issue itself

Because the brain can process words faster than a person can speak, there is extra time for the brain to think

It is the speaker's job to convince the audience to alter their viewpoint by proving that a policy is necessary

Spatial order

Monroe's motivated sequence

Multimedia presentation

Name-calling

Procedural needs

Process

Pronunciation

Vocal variety

A process which includes attention, need, satisfaction, visualization, and action to persuade a listener

When the main points of a speech are presented in a directional pattern

Words used with the intent of degrading or demeaning a group or person

A presentation which combines two or more types of visual aids

A system or series of actions which produce a result

The details of the conduct of a group, including location, agenda, and logistical issues

A method of making a speech expressive by using inflections and changes in rate

The accepted way to say a word, including the sound and rhythm of the word

Made in the USA
San Bernardino, CA
04 June 2020